SACRAMENTAL ETHICS

Timothy F. Sedgwick

SACRAMENTAL ETHICS
Paschal Identity and the
Christian Life

Fortress Press   Philadelphia

Library of Congress Cataloging-in-Publication Data

Sedgwick, Timothy.
   Sacramental ethics.

   Bibliography: p.
   1. Christian ethics—Anglican authors.
2. Sacraments. 3. Paschal mystery. I. Title.
BJ1241.S43   1987   241'.043   86–45925
ISBN 0–8006–1965–X

2667H86   Printed in the United States of America   1–1965

You are the Body of Christ; that is to say, in you and through you the method and work of the incarnation must go forward. You are to be taken, you are to be consecrated, broken and distributed, that you may become the means of grace and vehicles of the eternal charity.

St. Augustine

Contents

Preface

This book began to take written form in the spring of 1983 as I reworked my introductory course in Christian ethics. I had become increasingly convinced that worship in the Episcopal Church was the central place in which Christian faith was mediated and celebrated. *Lex orandi, lex credendi:* the law of worship or prayer is the law of belief. In other words, Christian faith and life is grounded in *orthodoxia,* a community formed in the praise and worship of God.[1] Any Christian theology and ethic within sacramental traditions such as Anglicanism must then have its grounding in worship.

My interest in worship and sacramental theology itself began a bit earlier. Upon coming to Seabury-Western Theological Seminary in 1978, I realized that despite work in rites and rituals from the perspective of anthropology and sociology, I had no theology of worship, at least in any self-conscious and systematic sense. I do not know the dominant reasons—whether out of intellectual interest, a desire to have some critical framework for entering into the range of discussions about what should be done in the worship at the seminary, or the sense of responsibility to students who would ask questions about the relationship between worship and ethics—but I soon began reading sacramental theology, at first along with a student who was taking a directed study under Leonel Mitchell, professor of liturgics at Seabury-Western. My understanding has increased as my conversations with Lee have continued, prompted in part from having taught jointly with Lee a course on the sacrament of reconciliation. Lee has also provided continual counsel, answering questions and insuring that my arguments regarding worship are adequately informed by the extensive work in liturgics and sacramental theology.

In 1980 I was also teaching a course in Anglican theology and ethics. I believe students need to understand their own tradition in order to appropriate and proclaim their faith. The voices of the tradition echo through a tradition; the question is whether or not such voices will be engaged consciously and therefore critically and constructively. In addition my interest in Anglican ethics was to discover what was normative, if not distinctive, about Anglicanism.

Theologies of Anglicanism most often have claimed that Anglicanism is the *via media* between Catholicism and Protestantism or that Anglicanism has a distinctive theological method that is grounded in appeals to Scripture, tradition, and reason. Such claims, however, are either so formal that they make no normative or distinctive claims or else they assume a particular content which is by no means normative for the tradition as a whole.[2] It became increasingly clear that any fundamental unity within the Anglican tradition would have to be prior to the particular theologies themselves; in fact, specific theologies within Anglicanism could be best understood as grounded in the worshiping community and animated by the need to resolve conflicts and deepen the meaning and life of faith.[3]

I soon began to include my developing understanding of worship and its relation to community and ethics as one part of the introductory course I teach in Christian ethics. My students have helped me think through this relation, both by their excitement when my thought made sense of their experience and by their silences and questions when further thought and greater clarification have been needed. The chapters of this book have also been prompted and developed in a broader conversation in the church. I am especially thankful to the Lay Academy of the Diocese of West Virginia for their invitation, and more especially for the ensuing conversation, to offer a five-day course on worship and the Christian life in the summer of 1983. A similiar opportunity was provided by the Leadership Training Program of the Diocese of Minnesota in the fall of 1984. Other individual lectures and presentations on various occasions to different groups have also been important. Most fundamental, however, have been the range of worshiping communities in the Episcopal church; they have given birth to this vision of the Christian life, grounded as it is in the worshiping community.

Intellectual debts are always great and varied. This makes it difficult to acknowledge only some debts without misleading the reader and embarrassing oneself. However, in recently reading through some of the writings of H. Richard Niebuhr and in reviewing a manuscript on Niebuhr, I was struck by how strongly I still resonate with his thought. While my work arises from a different context and is framed differently, Niebuhr's sense of the historicity of all of life and the corresponding social understanding of the self, his insight into the symbolic character of human knowing and action expressed in the image of responsibility, and his confessionalism that expresses Christian faith in terms of transformation from defensiveness to trust are abiding convictions deep within my mind. As an Anglican I have engaged Niebuhr's convictions most formatively through the thought of Frederick Denison Maurice, nineteenth-century Anglican divine and Niebuhr's exemplar par excellence of those who express the Christian position of Christ transforming culture. Most significant for my thought, Maurice has grounded Niebuhr's transformative stance within the Anglican context of the worshiping community of faith. [4]

The first full draft of this book was completed during a sabbatical in 1985 from Seabury-Western. Both during the sabbatical and since, the seminary has been most supportive of my work. The initial draft was given fuller form in light of a careful reading and lengthy discussion with Philip Turner. As part of a longer and broader conversation, Phil has sought to insure that my vision of the Christian life does not emphasize vision to the extent that it loses touch with a way of life that is distinctively Christian. The final draft was aided by a careful reading of the manuscript by Davis Perkins at Fortress Press. Davis was able to understand what I was trying to say and then indicate how my understanding of sacramental ethics might be clarified and amplified.

Others have been significant conversation partners aiding me in discovering what I think or at least what I need to think about. I especially give thanks for my sustained conversation with David Fisher; our ongoing exploration of language and transcendence informs my thought in ways far more significant than is evident. I also thank W. Taylor Stevenson for reading several sections of this manuscript and for more general support of my work. Larry Handwerk, Jim Crawford, and Alicia Crawford read drafts of the manuscript and have helped me hear what they heard in their readings; they then particularly helped me to see what I needed to say in a different way as well as what else I simply wanted to say. Shannon Jung and I talked about some of this work in its beginning stages; it was, though, in a more general conversation much later that he suggested the title for the book. The book is dedicated to Martha, Sarah, and Ellen because with them daily life is sustained and renewed.

TIMOTHY F. SEDGWICK
Seabury-Western Theological Seminary
Pentecost, 1986

NOTES

1. See Aidan Kavanagh, *On Liturgical Theology* (New York: Pueblo, 1984), 91, 92.

2. See Timothy F. Sedgwick, "Revisioning Anglican Moral Theology," *Anglican Theological Review* 63 no. 1 (January 1981): 1–20.

3. See Stephen Sykes, *The Identity of Christianity* (Philadelphia: Fortress Press, 1984), 282–86.

4. Most influential of Maurice's work has been *The Kingdom of Christ*, 2 vols., ed. Alec R. Vidler (London: SCM, 1958). For Niebuhr's presentation, see *Christ and Culture* (New York: Harper & Row, 1951), 218–29.

chapter 1

Introduction

Clifford Geertz tells the Indian story "about an Englishman who, having been told that the world rested on a platform which rested on the back of an elephant which rested in turn on the back of a turtle, asked . . . , what did the turtle rest on? Another turtle. And that turtle? 'Ah, Sahib, after that it is turtles all the way down.' "[1] What is true about the origins of our world is true about all beginnings, and Christian ethics is no exception. The question of what we should do and how we should form our lives raises additional questions. We act in certain ways because of the kind of people we are. Our identities, moreover, are formed by the communities in which we live. And then we are thrown back upon the history of our lives and the life of the community until finally "it is turtles all the way down."

To call an ethic Christian is to qualify an ethic and suggest reasons why we do what we do. And yet to call an ethic Christian is not self-explanatory. A first question is obviously what is meant by Christian. This leads to questions about Jesus Christ and God—for example, about the meaning of God and how Jesus Christ relates the believer to God. Every question begets both an answer and another question until one begins to repeat oneself. All arguments are in a sense circular; what is important, however, is how large the circle is. The larger the circle the more we can discern the fundamental reasons for the way we live and act.

Christian ethics must begin with God, specifically the question of how we come to know God and God's purposes. It is only by beginning theologically, by beginning with God, that we may deepen our under-

standing and relation to God in our daily lives. If we begin with moral
problems or with a set of moral principles we may illumine moral conflicts
and evaluate possible courses of action, but the concern of Christian
ethics is more than moral illumination or prescription. Most fundamentally, Christian ethics is concerned with the Christian life, with how we
are to discern God in our lives in light of Jesus Christ and, in turn, how
we are to form our lives in order to express and deepen our relationship
with God.

In order to speak about God it is necessary to describe an understanding
of God and God's purposes, specifically how God is experienced and
related to the events and relations that constitute the world. To move to
ethics is to move from what is perceived to what ought to be done. This
move from description to prescription is direct since the ultimacy of
religious faith means that believers desire to be in relation to God. In
light of the way in which God is perceived to be related to the world,
ethics describes the character and form of life that would express and
deepen the relationship with God. As James Gustafson expresses the
task of theological ethics: "We are to relate ourselves and all things in
a manner (or in ways) appropriate to their relations to God."[2]

How to begin with God, however, is not altogether clear. Some would
begin with Scripture while others would begin with the nature and
doctrine of God itself. The problem, of course, in beginning with either
of these two points is that they already presuppose the experience of
faith and a community of faith. Scripture and theology both, although
in different ways, arise from the life of a community and give expression
to their experience of God. It is the gathered community of worship that
forms the canon of Holy Scripture and determines what is normative
about the "charter documents" that express our faith. Specific theologies
likewise are dependent upon the community of faith as the community
seeks to give expression to faith in light of its history and experience.
What is true for Scripture and theology is also true for ethics. Developing
an understanding of God and God's purposes and the appropriate human
response presupposes the more fundamental experience of faith in the
Christian community.[3]

To foreshadow my argument, I am convinced that the place to begin
in understanding Christian faith and the Christian life is through the
worshiping community. Worship relates faith and life. In worship the
story of Christian faith is told, including both an understanding of God
and God's purposes and of the life in response to God. But worship does

more than express the meaning of Christian faith. As Aidan Kavanagh says, worship is a "transaction with reality."[4] In worship the participant is changed and formed in relation to God. To begin with worship and the worshiping community is to begin at the center of Christian faith in the experience of conversion and reconciliation. To grasp the formative experience of faith in worship is to find the basis for comprehending God and the character and form of the Christian life.

While worship promises a privileged point of entry into the Christian life, it is not insular. Worship itself is not self-explanatory. In one sense this entire book is directed at comprehending the axiom from liturgical theology: *lex ordandi, lex credendi*, or more accurately, *lex supplicandi legem statuat credendi*: the law of worship constitutes or founds the law of belief.[5] Of course understandings of God and the Christian life that arise from worship must make sense of the broader experience and understanding of God and the world. In this sense beliefs about God and the world that arise from worship are tested, modified, and confirmed in light of their ability to comprehend reality as a whole.

This understanding of worship reflects a corresponding view of language which I will develop in chapter 2. Fundamentally, language always both reveals and conceals, discloses and encloses, the world in which we live. The stories we tell do not correspond to reality. There is no master narrative that provides a blueprint of both the way things are and the way they ought to be. There is no knowledge apart from language, no unmediated and therefore immediate intuition of the way things are. Rather, the way in which worship effects conversion and reconciliation may be understood in terms of two functions of language, what may be called the mythic and the parabolic. In myth, stories explain the world and thereby mediate a world to the individual and the community. The stories we tell, however, inevitably become taken for granted as the way the world "is." The world is thereby circumscribed, and human life is cut off from other dimensions of reality. As with language in general, though, worship not only tells stories about God and provides a vision of life in relation to God. Worship is also parabolic, challenging the world of worshipers and thrusting them into a different relationship to God and the world, a relationship which for the believer is redemptive.

The privileged place of worship is not simply because worship expresses a vision of the Christian life. Rather, worship is privileged because in worship conversion and reconciliation are both celebrated and effected. In worship Christians not only proclaim and celebrate their reconciliation to reality; in worship Christians also experience and are conformed to reality. Worship embodies the movement of faith that animates all Christian understanding. Understanding this faith, however, is not self-evident; it is not given in worship itself. All understandings reflect other understandings of the world. Any articulation of faith is necessarily tested, modified, and confirmed by other understandings of reality. Still, since conversion and reconciliation are both expressed and effected in worship, worship is the place to begin in developing both theology and ethics, in developing an understanding of God and God's purposes and, correspondingly, the form of life that would express and deepen the relationship with God.

Chapters 3 and 4 move to what is central to worship and the Christian life, what I have called the paschal mystery, the paschal relationship, the paschal movement of faith, or the paschal character of faith. "Paschal" historically refers to Jesus' passion and resurrection. The paschal mystery, however, is not something that simply happened in the historical past that reveals knowledge about the meaning of life. Worship cannot be reduced to the stories told from Scripture, preached from the pulpit, or celebrated in the sacraments. In worship the worshiper participates in the paschal mystery. The fundamental reality of life is not only revealed, but the worshiper is reconciled to that reality.

Most simply described, this paschal movement is fourfold: acknowledgment of God, the opening and offering of ourselves, the experience of grace, and the formation of the community of faith in love and in the embrace of the world in all its travail. In the Eucharist this paschal movement is reflected and effected in the four parts of the liturgy—the liturgy of the Word, the offertory, the Great Thanksgiving, and the communion and dismissal—and most clearly in the reenacting of Jesus' passion and resurrection in the Great Thanksgiving. In this worship Christians proclaim that "by Christ, with Christ, and in Christ" they are delivered "from evil, . . . out of error into truth, out of sin into righteousness, out of death into life."[6]

Central to the paschal mystery is the understanding that we are not autonomous, self-sufficient beings capable of our own fulfillment, despite what much of contemporary culture suggests. We are not our own but are dependent upon those about us and the world-at-large. Our life is given in the families in which we first find ourselves, in our neighborhoods, among our friends, and through the social, economic, and political communities that secure our daily life, for better or worse. We are also dependent upon nature for our sustenance, from elemental needs of food and water to the many things we value for their beauty. We may deny these relationships but only at our own expense. To deny these relations is to withdraw from the world into a life we seek to fashion apart from our dependencies. Such a life may begin as an exciting and heroic vision but ends in a defensive fortress mentality where death itself stands as the final judgment of our lives. Alternatively, we can acknowledge the relations that form life and, in turn, form our life in accord with them. True worship effects this movement, both reconciling and forming the Christian.

At one level the argument about worship is descriptive; at another level it assumes an understanding of the symbolic character of language and acts developed in the second chapter. This symbolic character of worship is itself expressed by the medieval definition of sacrament as that which effects by signifying.[7] In worship the meaning of Jesus' life, ministry, passion, death, and resurrection is signified. But more than revealing meaning, worshipers participate in what is signified and thereby experience the paschal movement of faith in their own lives.

The centrality of worship for the Christian life and for developing an understanding of both Christian faith and the Christian life is a circular argument. The reason I begin with worship reflects an understanding of the symbolic nature of human meaning. This understanding of meaning reflects broader philosophical understandings of the world itself, for example, convictions about the social and historical character of human life. In turn, these convictions reflect understandings of the development of a tradition, including the formation of the canon of Scripture and the way theology functions within the community of faith. And, of course, such convictions are confirmed in my own experience of worship in a community of faith.

There is no way of simply beginning with worship and reading off from the "text" of worship an understanding of Christian faith and the Christian life. The adequacy of an argument may be judged only by the entire picture presented, by how well the circle is drawn and filled in. The adequacy of describing Christian faith in paschal terms depends on how well this description conveys what is essential to the experience of faith, the Christian tradition, beginning with the understanding of Jesus Christ conveyed in Scripture, and the broader experience and understanding of the world. As James Gustafson emphasizes, all theological arguments depend upon judgments about different sources that mutually inform each other: "(a) the historically identifiable sources of Christian thought, that is, the Bible and the Christian tradition; (b) philosophical methods, insights, and principles; (c) scientific information and methods that are relevant and about which there is little dispute; and (d) human experience broadly conceived."[8]

A paschal description of Christian faith and worship is, of course, not an exhaustive account. Many descriptions of faith and worship may be given. Worship consists of texts so thickly textured that any account may appear reductionistic. To claim that Christian faith and worship are fundamentally paschal in character is not, however, to deny other dimensions of meaning. Besides functioning in a range of ways—including psychologically, sociologically, and aesthetically—worship is always rooted in daily experiences and in the specific life of a community. No account of worship can express all of the many layers of meaning, especially as any meaning reflects the particular communities and individuals that gather together to worship, each with their own personal histories. The very elements in the Eucharist, bread and wine shared in a common meal, convey a range of meanings from the sense of our dependence upon nature and human toil to our common fellowship. As the body and blood of Jesus Christ, the eucharistic meal assumes additional layers of meaning as it recalls the history of Israel itself.[9]

To argue for the paschal character of worship is not to reduce worship and Christian faith to a univocal meaning but to express a normative vision of what is essential to the experience of worship and Christian faith. Only some such articulation provides a means of expressing the character of Christian faith in a manner that will enable the development of both a critical and constructive theological ethic. Ernst Troeltsch has classically expressed the nature of this task and the problems of such formulation. As he says, "The essence is an intuitive abstraction, a religious and ethical critique [of previous understandings], a flexible development concept [in understanding Christian faith] and the ideal to be applied in the work of shaping and recombining for the future." The danger of subjectivism is apparent but cannot be avoided. "Every . . . formulation of ideas and values is an individual, creative act which arises out of the possession and appropriation of previous acts, but which conscientiously shapes the development of what is possessed in such a way that in the new formation of values the acquisition of the past coincides with personal conviction, and the necessity of a driving idea within the development is united with the personal grasp of this idea."[10]

Again, all arguments have a circular character. What prevents them from being mere assertions is the scope of the circle. The normative idea of the paschal character of Christian faith grounded in worship may be viewed as the center of the circle with the discussion of language, worship, and the character of the Christian life filling in the actual area of the circle. While the area of the circle finds its center at one point, the center of the circle itself does not exist apart from the surrounding area.

In developing the understanding of worship in chapters 3 and 4 I want to emphasize that worship is more than ritual storytelling. More than conveying an understanding of reality, worship constitutes and establishes a way of life marked by the movement in response to God of opening and offering the self, the experience of grace, and the embrace of the world. In our contemporary world, however, worship has increasingly become separated from the rest of our lives until it is reduced to spiritualized exercise, moral exhortation, or simply an aesthetic experience incapable of effecting the movement of faith. The privatization of worship is reflected in understandings of sin and reconciliation. Understandings of sin are so highly individualized in the modern world that reconciliation is attempted by a private act of individual resolve or by exchange of forgiveness between individuals. This stands in sharp contrast to earlier understandings of worship and the Christian life. As the sacrament of reconciliation indicates, reconciliation depends upon taking on an identity: to be a Christian is to assume a way of life.

In the remaining chapters I want to turn attention from worship to the Christian moral life. The task of Christian ethics is to deepen the movement of faith which I have called paschal. It is, therefore, a mistake to think of Christian ethics exclusively in terms of casuistry, of resolving moral quandaries by analyses of various cases. While it is necessary to consider cases, Christian ethics is more broadly part of the task of the cure of souls, sustaining and nurturing individuals and the community in their faith. In this sense ethics is, as was traditionally the case, a practical discipline developed in conjunction with both ascetic theology and pastoral theology. Spiritual direction, pastoral care, and moral guidance all have as their primary objective sanctification, enabling Christians to deepen their faith by helping Christians form their lives in relation to God.

In order to accomplish its task a Christian ethic must relate the paschal movement of faith to the particular relations and conflicts that form our lives. The paschal movement of faith does not in itself provide the moral images for understanding and forming our relations in the world. The images by which we construe the meaning of our experience are taken from daily life. While informed by tradition, the choice of moral images represents a decision that must both reflect the fundamental paschal character of human life and illumine the particular relations themselves. The development of an ethic thereby provides a means of both developing and testing the adequacy of the paschal imagery as the essential revelation of the nature of reality. Chapters 5, 6, and 7 seek to delineate the character of such a Christian ethic by examining three areas: the interpersonal relations of human sexuality, the social sphere of friendship and the obligation to broader service, and the political domain of the use of force. Each of these areas gives expression to our identity. They are also areas fraught with conflict and choice. They thus provide the opportunity to reflect theologically and ethically in order to provide both guidance and understanding of the Christian life.

In envisioning our sexual identities and relations we need to begin with a broader understanding of what it is to be human. In dealing with sexuality, as in confronting any other area, if our ethic is to begin with our Christian identity we must begin with the underlying vision that frames our understanding of our relationship to the world itself. In chapter 5 I will argue that gift provides the central moral image for understanding our lives in light of Christian faith. Gift reflects the paschal mystery. Our life is not our own but is given by God. Death comes when we deny this fact and seek to build a world independent of the relations that form our life. Gift amplifies the moral response to the paschal movement of life by focusing our attention on the fact that life is given only in the embrace and care of the relationships that give and structure life.

Sexual relations are in this light not simply opportunities for immediate pleasure and self-fulfillment; rather, sexual relations are among the most intimate opportunities to embrace the gift of another, acknowledging our own dependence on the other while sharing and supporting them in their ongoing care of creation. In summary, the fundamental goods expressed in human sexuality are those of pleasure, mutuality, and generativity. The image of gift, moreover, helps us to see the mutual relationship between these goods: pleasure and mutual care are brought to fruition in a relationship in which persons are turned from themselves to the broader embrace and care for those beyond them.

Such an understanding of sexuality reflects the fundamental paschal character of life. We first suffer the relations and limits that form our lives. We respond by either denial or consent. Consent is to open ourselves to creation, to its power and possibilities. Here we experience the graciousness, the giftedness, of our lives and of being itself. In response we embrace and care for creation. At the center of this movement is forgiveness, for in forgiveness the atrophy of our lives and the bondage of our will are transformed by the sense of the gratuitousness of life. Human relations must reflect this paschal movement; they must have a form which conforms to the paschal movement. Description leads to prescription. There may, for example, be different expressions of sexuality, from that within the extended family in traditional or archaic society to the nuclear family of the modern world, from heterosexuals to homosexuals. However, each relation will have a common form which expresses and deepens the paschal relationship. In the area of sexuality this has meant a covenant relationship in which individuals commit themselves to love and care for the other for life, until death. It is this life commitment that expresses an unconditional acceptance of the other and thereby a love which is directed not at self-fulfillment but at an acknowledgment of the other as gift. Forgiveness in turn becomes a central virtue in marriage, as it is within all the relationships that form human life.

A normative vision does not preclude exceptions, for example the possibility of divorce. One may even argue about the vow of monogamy that has been central to Christian marriage. The task of Christian ethics, however, is to demand that any action expresses and deepens the experience of God. This necessitates an argument for a normative practice or, perhaps better expressed, a form of life. Only as we define ourselves in the relations that constitute human life do we make sense of our life and form our identity. Christian ethics is the discipline which seeks to provide an adequate and coherent account of the Christian life in relation to the experience and understanding of God. This provides not only guidance in practical moral decision-making. As importantly, Christian ethics provides a vision of reality grounded in God. In this way Christian ethics is an apology for faith that will deepen faith and enable response.

The need for an adequate moral vision in understanding the Christian life is well illustrated by attempts to see the moral life in the singular terms of love. The inadequacy of such accounts is evident when love is seen either as a disposition given in faith or as the essential content of the Christian life. As a disposition love has been viewed as enabling a person to discern intuitively what to do. As the essence of the Christian life love has been understood exclusively in terms of *agape*, love as self-sacrifice, what in Latin is *caritas* and from which comes the English "charity." Both accounts are reductionistic. Claims of intuition reinforce taken-for-granted cultural beliefs and convictions. To see love narrowly in terms of agape imposes a monism on reality that fails to apprehend the particular relations that form our life. In the seventeenth century Jeremy Taylor wrote, "When friendships were the noblest things in the world, charity was little."[11] The opposite is equally true. And life is not given apart from friendships and the other particular relationships in life.

In light of the paschal character of faith chapter 6 explores the meaning of love in terms of the contrast between love as eros and love as agape, between the images of friendship and servanthood, and between embracing and honoring particular relationships and the more universal call to embrace and care for all of creation. Such a broadened vision helps to discern a range of concerns and issues. For example, it helps grasp the tensions raised between male and female perspectives on the needs of the self and the tension between the place of friendship and work in our lives. How life is lived amidst these tensions, moreover, expresses and deepens the paschal movement of faith. How we love ourselves and love others or how we are both friends and servants expresses and nurtures our paschal faith: the opening of the self to the relationships that constitute life itself, the suffering of these particular relations, the experience of grace, and then a deeper and fuller embrace of creation itself.

As in the area of sexuality, the expression of love and friendship may vary. Certainly in traditional societies where marriage was more social and economic than romantic, friendships were at the very heart of society. With the rise of the nuclear family the place of friendships was narrowed, and many of the expectations for friendships were transferred to marriage. Life, however, atrophies without friends who share in and support broader activities and purposes. The development of friendship is not then simply a matter of personal taste. As the paschal character of Christian faith illumines, friendship is a significant aspect of life that is important to witness to and deepen faith itself.

The final practical example is taken from the political domain. The use of force raises specific, practical, moral questions; but, like sexuality and friendship, questions about the use of force raise even more fundamental questions about the form of the Christian life. This is most vividly expressed in the opposition between pacifists and just war theorists, between those who renounce the taking of the life of another and those who will take another's life in self-defense, in the defense of the innocent, or for the sake of justice. The question of the use of force is focused on the state since the state is founded on the use of force, both internally in maintaining order and externally in defense of itself against other nations. Pacifists and just war advocates see the Christian community in different relation to the state and, therefore, prescribe different ways of life.

Just war advocates express the conviction that justice is a precondition of peace, that the peace Christians seek is not simply the absence of killing but an order where respect is given to all people. The pacifist, on the other hand, reminds us that the meaning of peace is not given in a political future but is a living reality in which we are invited to participate.[12] Practically, the pacifist helps us see that to relegate peace to the future has not only failed to bring about a new order but has corrupted the warriors as well. The Christian vocation is rather, from the pacifist perspective, to be peaceful now and thereby witness to the ultimate relationship between individuals and the rest of the world.

Both just war theorists and pacifists reflect strands of the Christian tradition. Both have their own integrity and together express the fundamental tension of living out the Christian faith in a way which does not take us out of the world but calls us to care for the world and to witness to its ultimate character. The problem of peace and the use of force then points back to Christian identity and the community of faith. While it is possible to argue for one or the other stance, the more fundamental need is for a theology of peace which would indicate more fully the form of the Christian life. As the Roman Catholic bishops' pastoral letter on peace indicated, a theology of peace has yet to be developed.[13] The problem with attempts to develop such a theology is that peace itself is a far too general and therefore abstract an image. What is required are moral images that will construe the relations that form the Christian life and which result in peace. Such moral reflection will not resolve the conflict between just war advocates and pacifists, but it will help to express what is distinctive about the Christian life and community.

These three moral investigations of human sexuality, friendship and service, and the use of force are not intended to be exhaustive or even complete. Rather, though, they should mark the form of the Christian life in personal, social, and political spheres. The central argument is that the fundamental character of life is paschal. Christians proclaim their conversion and reconciliation through the community that celebrates this life as signified and effected in the life, death, and resurrection of Jesus Christ. The meaningfulness, integrity, and vitality of worship rests upon coherence between life lived and celebrated. This requires Christians to conform their lives to the paschal form of life. The task of Christian ethics is to describe this life.

This ethic may be called a sacramental ethic as it is grounded in the sacramental worship of the church. It is also sacramental in that the ethic is a vision of the Christian life which signifies the meaning of paschal in the relations and conflicts of daily life and thereby enables such a life. In this sense, a Christian ethic that successfully fulfills its task will not only provide practical guidance but, in discerning the meaning of the paschal movement of faith in human life, will deepen faith and form the church as God's continuing sacrament in the world. As sacramental, Christian ethics is integral to faith. Without a moral vision Christian faith becomes divorced from daily life, the world becomes alien to faith, and so faith itself becomes spiritualized and often aesthetic. A moral vision alone enables the sanctification of time and space, of daily life, where humans in fact dwell. Anything less denies the Christian proclamation of the incarnation and so the conviction that redemption is always redemption of creation itself.

NOTES

1. Clifford Geertz, "Thick Description: Towards an Interpretive Theory of Culture," *The Interpretation of Cultures: Selected Essays* (New York: Basic Books, 1973), 28, 29.

2. James M. Gustafson, *Ethics from a Theocentric Perspective*, vol. 2, *Ethics and Theology* (Chicago: Univ. of Chicago Press, 1984), 2.

3. See Sykes, *The Identity of Christianity*, 276–80.

4. Kavanagh, *On Liturgical Theology*, 88.

5. See Kavanagh, *On Liturgical Theology*, 91, 92; also see Geoffrey Wainwright, *Doxology: The Praise of God in Worship, Doctrine and Life* (New York: Oxford Univ. Press, 1980), 218–83.

6. *The Book of Common Prayer* (New York: Church Hymnal Corp. and Seabury Press, 1977), 368. This analysis of conversion and reconciliation as grounded in worship is itself grounded in the nature and experience of worship in the Anglican

church. The centrality and common form of eucharistic worship in other sacramental traditions, such as the Roman Catholic church and the Lutheran church, make the argument of this book clearly applicable to these traditions. The extent to which the shape of the liturgy and the corresponding understanding of conversion and reconciliation are shared in common with nonsacramental forms of worship is an important and open question.

7. See Karl Rahner, "Introductory Observations on Thomas Aquinas' Theology of the Sacraments in General," *Theological Investigations* (London: Darton, Longman & Todd, 1976), 14:149–60.

8. James M. Gustafson, *Protestant and Roman Catholic Ethics* (Chicago: Univ. of Chicago Press, 1978), 142.

9. See David N. Power, *Unsearchable Riches: The Symbolic Nature of Liturgy* (New York: Pueblo, 1984), esp. 127–30, 154–64.

10. Ernst Troeltsch, "What Does 'Essence of Christianity' Mean?" *Writings on Theology and Religion*, trans. and ed. Robert Morgan and Michael Pye (London: Duckworth, 1977), 164, 166; see also 156–70. For further discussion of the heuristic character of "essence," see Sykes, *The Identity of Christianity*, 148–73 on Troeltsch, and 219–30 on three motives in identifying the "essence of Christianity": "simplification, the creation of priorities, and the problem of continuity" (p. 220).

11. Jeremy Taylor, "Discourse on the Nature and Offices of Friendship," *Works*, vol. 1, ed. R. Heber, revised by C. P. Eden (London, 1847), 72; quoted in Gilbert C. Meilaender, *Friendship: A Study in Theological Ethics* (Notre Dame: Univ. of Notre Dame Press, 1981), 1.

12. David Hollenbach, S. J., *Nuclear Ethics* (New York: Paulist Press, 1983), 23.

13. National Conference of Catholic Bishops, *The Challenge of Peace: God's Promise and Our Response* (Washington, D.C.: United States Catholic Conference, 1983), 8.

chapter 2
Language, Worship, and Reality

In a hauntingly contemporary manner, Augustine in his *Confessions* foreshadows the question of how it is that we come to consciousness of God. Once I am conscious of the fact that the past and future are only present to me in memory and anticipation and that the present itself is focused by the remembered past and anticipated future, there is no immediate knowledge of God.[1] All of reality is mediated through our memories. Our understandings of reality, therefore, reflect our distinctive experiences and perspectives imbedded in language. There is no "pure" knowledge or language of God. Worship itself provides no pristine experience or knowledge of God. Worship can only give expression to our faith and effect that faith as worship constitutes an experience or exchange with reality. Before we begin with worship and specific claims about the experience and meaning of God, the broader understanding of the nature and relation of language and human experience may be helpfully developed.

The focus on language and experience is among the most general characteristics of modern philosophy, beginning with Descartes and intensifying with the turn to the subject associated with Kant.[2] Rather than rehearse this history, I want to focus the question on language, experience, and meaning through the work of John Dominic Crossan, a contemporary biblical scholar. Crossan is particularly helpful because his concern is theological: to understand how a text is related, or better relates us, to God.[3]

Crossan sees language as mediating reality. Language is what links us to reality. We grow up in a linguistic world. Language directs us and points us into the world as well as providing the means of our own self-expression. And language—whether the signified act or words them-selves—is the only public means we have of articulating and thereby sharing our experience of the world; it is, then, the only means we have to approach questions to God.[4]

In *The Dark Interval* Crossan emphasizes two functions of language: mediating and reconciling the diverse and conflicting experiences that constitute human life, and challenging such mediation and reconciliation in order to thrust the hearer back into the diverse and conflicting experiences themselves. The first function of language is mythic; the second function is parabolic. Myth, as Paul Ricoeur defines it, is "a traditional narration which relates to events that happened at the beginning of time and which has the purpose of providing grounds for ritual actions of people today and, in a general manner, establishing all the forms of action and thought by which humans understand themselves in their world."[5] What presses the narration forward is a set of opposites or differences. As the plot unfolds conflict increases until there is some resolution. Expressed in the terms of the French structuralists, "In every myth system we will find a persistent sequence of binary discriminations as between human/superhuman, mortal/immortal, male/female, legiti-mate/illegitimate, good/bad . . . followed by a 'mediation' of the paired categories thus distinguished."[6] In short, says Crossan, "Myth performs the specific task of mediating irreducible opposites."[7]

In contrast to myth is parable. Crossan defines a parable as a paradox formed into a story which reverses its audience's expectations and therefore stands as the binary opposite of myth. In other words, parables are a narrative sequence of binary discriminations in which the character of the irreducible opposites is heightened. The double function of parable parallels that of myth, as its opposite: parables create contradiction with a given situation of complacent security and, moreover, challenge the fundamental principle of reconciliation itself.[8]

Language obviously functions in other ways as well. Like the text of the eucharistic prayers, a narrative may have many levels of meaning, one playing off the meaning of the other, from the mundane and personal to the abstract and cosmic.[9] The contrast between myth and parable, however, well describes the dialectical relationship between language and experience. Language both expresses and construes our reality; it both voices our experience and effects new experiences of the world. Worship, likewise, as the traditional definition of sacrament says, effects by signifying.

Christian Scripture itself provides the primary text that functions both mythically and parabolically. The fundamental myth begins in the creation story in Genesis and develops in different ways in the various strands of tradition. In the priestly account that begins Genesis (Gen. 1:1—2:4a), the binary opposites are order and chaos. Order is understood as given in creation, as the consequence of God giving form to the void by creating light from darkness, separating sky from water, and then separating water to form the land. And so the creation proceeded until God completed it on the sixth day.

The theological tradition has understood such creation as creation *ex nihilo*, creation out of nothing. The account more accurately reflects the presence of chaos and the creation of order from chaos. What is clear is that order is created from chaos by a sovereign God. There is here a myth, a narrative in which two primordial elements of life, chaos and order, are brought to consciousness and understood by placing them in the context of some ultimate purposefulness. Through this the primordial sense of chaos and order are mediated to us; they are brought to our consciousness and reconciled. Chaos makes sense and is therefore no longer threatening. We may experience it, but within the myth it is domesticated by being understood in the broader context of God's purposefulness.

In the Yahwist account of creation (Gen. 2:4b—3:24) Adam and Eve succumb to the temptations of the serpent and in disobedience to God's command eat the fruit from the tree of knowledge. Cast out from the Garden men and women suffer in this world and ultimately are doomed to death. This story provides a second narrative of our origins. In this account the two binary opposites of good and evil are raised to consciousness and mediated. These two are mediated by understanding that, ultimately, evil is something we do to ourselves, we bring upon ourselves. Hence, suffering is the consequence of evil. Suffering and all natural evils are thereby explained: they make sense of the consequence of our sinfulness. This interiorization of evil, the making of evil a matter of human responsibility, ultimately subordinates evil to the good by understanding evil in terms of the corruption of the good. In this we have what Paul Ricoeur calls the Adamic myth.[10] The primordial experiences of being in the world are brought to consciousness and reconciled in terms of some broader and more universal meaning.

The Adamic myth is the primary myth that constitutes the Hebraic-Christian tradition. It is not, however, without a number of variations and dissent. The Deuteronomic historian sets out, for example, the meaning of the history of the Hebrew people in terms of covenant—perhaps more accurately a treaty—between God and the people of God. Basically, in the context of a covenant, the narrative is pressed forward in light of the people's disobedience and punishment, repentance and forgiveness. And the story continues over and over. The binary opposites of good and evil remain. Evil is explained in terms of human responsibility. Evil, particularly natural evil and suffering, is a consequence of human iniquity. It is compared to the punishment that a father gives his children, punishment as the means of education. The experience of good and evil is in this way brought to consciousness. As evil is under the broader purposes of God, good and evil are themselves reconciled.

What is designated as 2 Isaiah (Isa. 40—55) provides a striking contrast with the Deuteronomic historian in the way in which the Adamic myth is both affirmed and modified. By the time of the Babylonian exile of the Israelites it became increasingly untenable simply to assert that evil was a consequence of unfaithfulness. As raised for our age by the Holocaust, the issue could not be understood in terms of divine justice in which those who do good prosper and those who do evil suffer. The Book of Lamentations clearly evidences the problem of undeserved evil. Second Isaiah deals with this challenge by heightening still further human responsibility for evil. Basically the writer calls for a suffering servant who will freely accept the sufferings of the world and thereby reconcile not only himself or herself (or themselves) and the Hebrew people, but all people to God (esp. Isa. 52:13—53:12). If someone or a people can accept suffering they can transform it. If someone—despised, tormented, disfigured—can still embrace God then evil and suffering are made transitory; they are part of a transition, a movement by which we can grow in our capacity to know God. Suffering in fact becomes the vehicle by which God may be manifest. And if God is manifest in suffering itself then God is fully revealed as sovereign, so present in and through all creation.

Here in 2 Isaiah the Adamic myth is stretched to the extreme. Good and evil in their opposition are clearly made conscious. They are mediated and reconciled by the good will sufficient to embrace the evil and suffering itself. However, resolving the conflict at this one level leaves unanswered the conflict that was previously resolved in terms of God's purposefulness. The very success at bringing to consciousness the irreducible opposition between good and evil makes impossible resolving the problem in terms of God's purposefulness within history itself. The righteous simply do not prosper, and the evil do not suffer their just desert. There is simply no divine scale of justice on earth, in history. To believe this, to know this, is to be more fully conscious of the experience of evil and good. But, at the level of purpose, the question remains, "Why is there evil in the first place?"

Chaos and so meaninglessness threaten once more. The writer of 2 Isaiah in fact recalls this sense of chaos in reciting the action of God as creator of the world out of chaos (Isa. 40:12–31); however, the end of it all, since it cannot be resolved within history, must be resolved beyond history. If some such resolution of good and evil cannot be accomplished the myth fails, at least as the one true story that corresponds to reality, as the master story that explains and predicts the true nature of things. So, as Georg Föhrer says, Isaiah becomes the "first eschatological prophet."[11]

This extended example indicates both the nature and the general character of the myth of the Hebraic tradition. All of these narratives relate events that bring to consciousness irreducible opposites that constitute the fundamental experience that we have as humans in the world. The myth raises these experiences to consciousness so that they can be grasped and embraced in our own lives. The myth is able to do this through a narrative that reconciles the opposition in terms of some broader purpose. Crossan states this dual character of myth in similar fashion. Myth, says Crossan, provides for "the reconciliation of an individual contradiction; this, though, is possible only with the belief in the permanent possibility of reconciliation."[12]

The differences between the Priestly, Deuteronomic, Yahwist, and Prophetic accounts evidence the diversity of tradition. The Hebraic-Christian tradition is not uniform; there is no singular myth that insures the reconciliation of the conflicting aspects of experience. In fact, the tradition is often a critique of itself and in this way functions parabolically. The myths taken for granted are challenged by new understandings. For example, the Book of Ezekiel first introduces the claim that individuals are responsible for their own lives and not the lives of their forebears. It was illegitimate, therefore, to justify suffering—to reconcile suffering with a sense of the fundamental goodness of creation—by claiming that human suffering is for the sins of those before us. To achieve a new reconciliation between good and evil, given the perduring experience of suffering, eventually demands the eschatological vision expressed in 2 Isaiah. But apart from the new variation in the myth, Ezekiel first contradicts the myth of the people, challenges the fundamental principle of reconciliation, and thereby heightens the sense of the conflicting, irreducible experiences of human life, of good and evil, order and chaos, legitimate and illegitimate. This indicates the parabolic, the use of language to reverse expectations and place the hearer again more centrally in the experiences that animated the myth in the first place. What is distinctive about parables as such is that they do not attempt reconciliation but leave the hearer in the fundamental tension of life itself.

Perhaps the greatest examples of parables are those of Jesus. Some of these are stories told and others are actions within his own life. In each case the story or the act contradicts the expectations of the listeners and thereby brings to consciousness the opposites that had been taken for granted. For example, Jesus claims that the kingdom of God is like a mustard seed. The mustard seed is small and the mustard tree is actually a rather scraggly shrub. The listeners likely remembered this brief story—hence it was passed down and finally written down—because it surprised them, shocked them, and scandalized them. The kingdom of God was traditionally referred to in terms of the cedars of Lebanon. The kingdom was thereby associated with something of regal stature. And here was a man claiming that the kingdom of God was like a mustard seed. The tension between God's reign and the sense of human fulfillment was thereby raised to consciousness without resolution.[13]

The parable of the prodigal son (Luke 15:11–24, 32) provides a more extended example. While the story tells of repentance, what probably was most striking to the early hearers was the response of the father to the return of his son. The father appears to have been waiting or at least longing for his son. He sees him a long way off. And then, unlike the response that would be expected of a Near Eastern man, the father responds in excess: He runs to meet his son. He flings his arms around him. He kisses him. Such acts would appear most undignified. Finally the father gives the son a robe and a ring, symbols of honor and authority, and the feast begins. To hear this story was surely to call into question expectations of reward and punishment and thereby what matters and how we should respond. The moralism that stands so deep within the Hebraic-Christian myth—especially as voiced in the Deuteronomic tradition—is challenged, complacent security is gone, and what finally holds life together is an open question.[14]

Parables raise to consciousness the primordial experiences that constitute our life in the world by raising the contradictions between our experience in the world and the accepted myths. In contrast to myth, parables restore before us, they raise to consciousness, the irreducible opposites that constitute the primordial experiences we have of ourselves in the world. As Crossan succinctly says, "Myth establishes world. . . , parable subverts the world."[15] The need for parables arises as the purposefulness of the world, the conviction of God's plan for us, becomes so taken for granted that we become distant from our world and live life abstractly or defensively. Myth no longer mediates reality; or, more accurately, myth no longer mediates between us and reality, drawing us to reality and reconciling us in that relation.

For Christians the ultimate parable is Jesus' crucifixion. The Messiah, the bearer of God's reign, was crucified. The conclusion could only be that this was not the Messiah. Crucifixion was after all a sign of judgment and rejection. This shock, however, became a revelation. The folly of the cross confirmed the folly of the parables themselves. The disciples experienced here in and through the crucifixion the risen Lord. The death of Jesus destroyed all of their remnant hopes for the kingdom they had envisioned; instead they encountered God and so God's reign in this man Jesus as they ate together and as he embraced the cross. No wonder, as Crossan says, that "the cross replaced the parables and became in their place the supreme Parable."[16]

This understanding of how human life is given in language helps to illumine the character of worship as well as the task of Christian ethics. In worship the stories of faith are told in the reading of the Scripture and in preaching and are enacted in a range of liturgies, including the central liturgies of Baptism and Eucharist. Mythically the stories continue to constitute a world; parabolically they challenge and dissolve the worlds we take for granted. As language has two sides—to reveal meaning and to challenge what has been taken for granted—worship has two sides. Worship expresses as well as challenges and transforms the relations of everyday life. Worship confirms and deepens previous insights while challenging the status quo. In this sense worship and daily life mirror each other, although the reflections never fully coincide. The end of such worship, however, is not intellectual insight. Worship mediates reality, both mythically and parabolically, and thereby brings the participant into relationship with reality, what Christians call God.

Christian ethics arises in the discrepancy between the sense of a redeemed life, celebrated in worship, and the actual relations that constitute daily life. The task of ethics then is to envision the Christian life in terms of the particular relations and conflicts of daily life. In this way practical moral reasoning—whether systematic or more like the folk wisdom of a people—seeks to sanctify daily life by relating it to God. Ethics is sacramental as it signifies and deepens the meaning of Christian faith in the world.

The distinctiveness of such an understanding of ethics may be illustrated by contrast with two dominant ethical stances in the West, intellectualism and voluntarism.[17] The intellectualist position has its classic expression in Platonic idealism and Aristotle's naturalism; it is reflected in the Christian tradition most notably in Thomism. This stance assumes that the myths, narratives, and propositions we tell ourselves correspond to reality. From this perspective there is a master story or a series of propositions that reveal an immutable order which expresses the way life should be.

In reaction to this intellectualism is voluntarism. This is expressed in the thought of mystics, medieval nominalists, in some of the primary assumptions of Reformation thinkers, most notably Martin Luther, by certain existentialists such as Søren Kierkegaard, and, in our century, by some neo-orthodox theologians. Voluntarists acknowledge that there is no correspondence between human thought and reality. Narratives and beliefs are human reflections that construe experience, needs, and desires. Meaning is always a human artifice and in that sense artificial. Rather than understanding reality in terms of a rational, knowable will, the voluntarist sees at the heart of reality a will or power which transcends rational categories. While this acknowledges the problem of intellectualism, voluntarism's rejection of human reason results in a naive intuitionism or the assertion of an authoritative, divine revelation and moral code that stands beyond reason. In either case assumptions about God's will are uncritically assumed.

To acknowledge our linguistic and historical constitution prevents either an intellectualist or voluntarist ethic. Our historical conditioned-ness—evidenced first by biblical criticism and now pressed home by world religions as well as by social-scientific descriptions of human action—prevents a return to an intellectualist stance where moral principles and rules can simply be read off nature as "the way things are." While that tradition provides a powerful witness to Christian faith, it is itself time-bound, conditioned by a metaphysic that is inadequate to comprehend the world as we know it.[18] Not only is reason incapable of grasping some eternal order, but modern cosmological theories based on the "big bang" are simply at odds with the cosmology of Aristotle and neo-Platonism. As the intellectualists emphasize, the moral life is purposeful, the formation of human life in order to achieve meaning and wholeness in life. But the intellectualists are wrong when they believe that a specific way of life is clearly given to reason.

Voluntarism, with its emphasis on the will and religious faith as a matter of trust, provides a refuge for those disillusioned with reason. But the still, small voice of God is not so clear as the voluntarist tradition would suggest. As the voluntarists often claim, the experience of God is the experience of trust as we come to sense the graciousness, the giftedness, of all that is. But this sense of trust does not yield the intuition of what ought to be done in the world.

Both intellectualists and voluntarists fail to comprehend the historical character of human life and the understanding of language as construing experience and orienting and relating us to reality. They both fail to acknowledge what is central to human life: thoroughly historical humans find their being in language. Language mediates reality as it both creates and dissolves the boundaries between the self and the world, as expressed in the understanding of the mythic and parabolic character of language. H. Richard Niebuhr gave classic expression to this understanding of human life in the image of the responsible self.[19] Given such an understanding, the Christian moral life is not primarily a determination of specific rules of conduct. Nor is the Christian life a matter of intuitively responding to the will of God. Rather the moral life for the Christian is fundamentally a matter of imagination and interpretation in order to develop a way of life that deepens the relation to God and bears witness to Christian faith in daily life. Christian ethics then is the attempt to relate all things to God through interpreting, evaluating, and imagining forms of life.

In order for an ethic to begin with God it is necessary to center upon the experience of God. Whatever interpretive claims are central to an understanding of God, such claims are means of construing of experience.[20] Because worship celebrates our experience of God—from judgment to conversion and reconciliation—Christian ethics may begin with God by beginning with a fuller analysis of the experience and meaning of worship. To this point something of the character of worship has been indicated. Worship is mythic as it mediates between the worshiper and reality; it is also parabolic as it dissolves the taken for granted attitudes and perceptions that distance the self from reality. In other words, worship mediates reality and relates us to God as it expresses and challenges our relation to reality and, in turn, celebrates and effects that relation. In the introduction I claimed that the "content" of this relation is paschal in character. A Christian ethic must then have at its center the development of the moral images that will reflect that paschal relation in daily life and relations. But what has still to be developed is the central claim that worship and Christian faith may be best understood in paschal terms. What cannot be forgotten, however, is that the development of such an ethic is the work of moral imagination in the community of faith.

NOTES

1. In Book 11 of his *Confessions*, translated by John K. Ryan (Garden City, N.Y.: Doubleday & Co., 1960), Augustine provides the first account in Western thought of time consciousness and thereby suggests implicitly the primacy of the subject in all knowing. Yet Augustine himself never raised the question about knowledge and God because of the overriding assumption that language corresponds to reality beyond time itself. "Wherever they are, and whatever they are, [future and past] do not exist except as present things. However, when true accounts of the past are given, it is not the things themselves, which have passed away, that are drawn forth from memory, but words conceived from their images. These images [of the things themselves are] implanted in the mind like footsteps as they passed through the senses" (Bk. 11, chap. 18, p. 291). See Charles Norris Cochrane, *Christianity and Classical Culture* (London: Clarendon Press, 1940), chap. 11, esp. 437–42.

2. On the turn to the subject see David Tracy, *Blessed Rage for Order* (New York: Seabury Press, 1975), 172–74. For a description of the challenge of psychoanalysis and semiology to the philosophy of the subject that continues to demand the move to the subject (to the *cogito*) in order to approach the question of being, see Paul Ricoeur, "The Question of the Subject," in *The Conflict of Interpretation*, ed. Don Ihde (Evanston: Northwestern Univ. Press, 1974), 236–66.

3. On the development of Crossan's thought, see David H. Fisher, "The Pleasures of Allegory," *Anglican Theological Review* 66 no. 3 (July 1984): 298–307. Crossan's understanding, approached through the parables, is reflected as well in the works of Dan O. Via, Jr., *The Parables: Their Literary and Existential Dimensions* (Philadelphia: Fortress Press, 1967); Sallie McFague, *Speaking in Parables* (Philadelphia: Fortress Press, 1975); Robert W. Funk, *Parables and Presence* (Philadelphia: Fortress Press, 1982); and Amos N. Wilder, *Jesus' Parables and the War of Myths* (Philadelphia: Fortress Press, 1982). While biblical scholarship has been dominated by a concern for the historical, implying that meaning is given by a "factual" referent, as these works on parables suggest, meaning is more fundamentally

constituted in the structure of the text and in the interaction of text and reader that literary theory has analyzed. For a recent examination of these questions with particular attention to the relation between structure and history, the reception and transmission of the text, and the problem of reference see Bernard C. Lategan and Willem S. Vorster, *Text and Reality: Aspects of Reference in Biblical Texts* (Philadelphia: Fortress Press; and Atlanta: Scholars Press, 1985).

4. " 'Reality' is the world we create in and by our language and our story so that what is 'out there,' apart from our imagination and without our language, is as unknowable as, say, our fingerprints, had we never been conceived. . . . I am claiming that what we know *is* reality here together and with each other" (John Dominic Crossan, *The Dark Interval: Towards a Theology of Story* [Niles, Ill.: Argus, 1975], 40).

5. Paul Ricoeur, *The Symbolism of Evil*, trans. Emerson Buchanan (Boston: Beacon Press, 1967), 5.

6. Edmund Leach, *Genesis as Myth and Other Essays* (London: Jonathan Cape, 1969) on Claude Lévi-Strauss, p. 11, quoted in Crossan, *The Dark Interval*, 51. On Lévi-Strauss see his "The Structural Study of Myth," *Structural Anthropology*, vol. 1, trans. Claire Jacobson and Brooke Grundfest Schoepf (New York: Basic Books, 1963), 206–31.

7. Crossan, *Dark Interval*, 51.

8. Ibid., 54–57. On the iconoclastic use of language to create silence see Susan Sontag, "The Aesthetics of Silence," *A Susan Sontag Reader* (New York: Farrar, Straus and Giroux, 1982). "Even if the artist's medium is words, he can share in this task: language can be employed to check language, to express muteness. Mallarme thought it was the job of poetry, using words, to clear up our world clogged reality—by creating silences around things. Art must mount a full-scale attack on language itself, by means of language and its surrogates, on behalf of the standard of silence" (p. 196).

9. See Crossan, *Raid on the Articulate: Cosmic Eschatology in Jesus and Borges* (New York: Harper & Row, 1976), esp. 115–31. See his *In Parables: The Challenge of the Historical Jesus* (New York: Harper & Row, 1973), 8–15, for Crossan's earlier, romantic distinction between image and idea. As Robert Scholes and Robert Kellogg claim, "This invidious distinction sees symbolism as being organic, nonintellectual, pointing to some mystical connection between the mind of the poet and the unreal world which is the shaping mind or soul behind actuality, wearing what we call the 'real' world as its vestment" (*The Nature of Narrative* [New York: Oxford Univ. Press, 1966], 106, 107, quoted in *Raid on the Articulate*, 116).

10. See Ricoeur, *The Symbolism of Evil*, 232–78.

11. Georg Föhrer, *Introduction to the Old Testament*, trans. David E. Green (Nashville: Abingdon Press, 1968), 383.

12. Crossan, *Dark Interval*, 56, 57.

13. See ibid., 93–96.

14. See McFague, *Speaking in Parables*, 12–17.

15. Crossan, *Dark Interval*, 59.

16. Ibid., 125.

17. As typifications, the stances of intellectualism, voluntarism, and the responsible self highlight central features of particular thinkers. Individual thinkers are invariably more nuanced, often including features from a different typical stance. Typical answers themselves are dependent upon judgments about a range of sources, for example, scriptural, historical, moral, theological, social-scientific, natural-scientific, and metaphysical. On intellectualism and voluntarism see Frederick A. Olafson, *Principles and Persons* (Baltimore: Johns Hopkins Univ. Press, 1967), 4–33. Also see Gustafson, *Protestant and Roman Catholic Ethics*, esp. 144–59.

18. See Gustafson, *Protestant and Roman Catholic Ethics*, 148–50, 152–53; *Ethics from a Theocentric Perspective*, vol. 1, *Theology and Ethics* (Chicago: Univ. of Chicago Press, 1981) 257–64; and vol. 2, *Ethics and Theology*, 53–60.

19. H. Richard Niebuhr, *The Responsible Self* (New York: Harper & Row, 1963), esp. 90–107, 149–60.

20. On language as construing experience, see John E. Smith, *Experience and God* (New York: Oxford Univ. Press, 1968), 46–56.

chapter 3

Worship and
Paschal Identity

Understanding how language mediates reality, forming and transforming our relation to the world, indicates at a formal level the integral relation between worship and daily life. I want, however, to move to the essential character of Christian faith and from within it develop the character of the Christian life.[1] My primary claim is that Christian faith is paschal in character, that the paschal movement is expressed and effected in Christian worship, and that Christian worship and daily life must mirror each other.[2]

While I want to argue for the paschal character of Christian faith through a description of Christian worship, something of the meaning that paschal has had for the worshiper first needs to be described. Historically paschal refers to the Jewish Passover which celebrates the Israelites' sacrifice of a lamb to God in Egypt, smearing blood on the house posts so that God would pass over them in order to punish the Egyptians and deliver them from slavery. This is remembered, reenacted, each week on the Sabbath. The Jew says, "We are these people." The weekly seder is hence an act of remembrance and identification. It is also an act of praise and thanksgiving, and an offering and commitment of the Jews to God.

For Christians, though, the word paschal refers to more than the Exodus narrative. In the words proclaimed at the Eucharist just before Christians share in communion: "Christ our Passover is sacrificed for us; therefore let us keep the feast." Paschal recalls the history of ancient Israel, but Christians do so only in light of what is for them the true paschal sacrifice, Jesus Christ. Again, as expressed in the Easter liturgy,

Jesus Christ is the "true paschal lamb." "By him, with him, and in him" is given the real passover from death to life.[3] As Christians have claimed for themselves, life is given in these events; they have the power to pass us over from death in our lives into God. At the most basic level, for the Christian paschal itself connotes Jesus' passion, his suffering and crucifixion, and his resurrection.

Here is sacrifice, not as an end in itself but as the offering of Jesus' life to God in praise and thanksgiving. This reflects the original meaning of the word "sacrifice," to "make" a thing sacrum, to pass it over altogether into the possession of God. Sacrifice has been a means of petition for divine favor. Such bargaining is exemplified by the sacrifice of Iphigenia to Artemis in order to set sail for Troy. The primary meaning of sacrifice, however, is to offer oneself to God. Like worship itself, sacrifice is fundamentally an act of remembrance and acknowledgment, offering and commitment, done in praise and thanksgiving.[4]

Of course, as the disciples found—not only between the cross and the resurrection but after their experience of the resurrection itself—the meaning of Jesus' sacrifice is not self-evident. In order to develop the essence of this paschal sacrifice I want to begin with the Christian rite of initiation, since here Christians give their first liturgical expression of faith. On the basis of this description I want to move to a broader description of what I shall call the paschal movement of faith effected in worship.[5]

In the early church what are now three sacraments—Baptism, Confirmation, and Communion—were three aspects of the rite of initiation.[6] After "education" in the faith as a member of the catechumenate a person was baptised. In response to the gospel he or she renounced Satan, the evil powers of this world, and all sinful desires and turned to Jesus Christ and promised to follow and obey him.[7] In the prayer of thanksgiving over the baptismal waters, the church expresses its understanding of what happens in baptism:

> We thank you, Almighty God, for the gift of water. Over it the Holy Spirit moved in the beginning of creation. Through it you led the children of Israel out of their bondage in Egypt into the land of promise. In it your Son Jesus received the baptism of John and was anointed by the Holy Spirit as the Messiah, the Christ to lead us, through his death and resurrection, from the bondage of sin into everlasting life.

> We thank you, Father, for the water of Baptism. In it we are buried with Christ in his death. By it we share in his resurrection. Through it we are reborn by

the Holy Spirit. Therefore in joyful obedience to your Son, we bring into his
fellowship those who come to him in faith, baptizing them in the Name of the
Father, and of the Son, and of the Holy Spirit.[8]

As the prayer indicates, the paschal mystery promises new life which is
confirmed and completed in acceptance and participation in the community of faith. This is signified by the passing of the peace and joining
in the eucharistic celebration of the community.

As the interrelationship between Baptism, Confirmation, and the
Eucharist suggests, the paschal action from death to life is not completed
in the rite of Baptism but is the character of the Christian life. In other
words, the paschal mystery is not so much something believed in as
something entered into. One does not so much become a Christian as
one is always in the process of becoming a Christian. The meaning of
paschal is not then simply defined. What is necessary is a description
of a way of life which begins from Christ's death and resurrection and
is continued in the Christian community itself.[9] This is precisely what
the church has claimed is effected in worship. Again, we may, therefore,
approach the meaning of paschal and thereby the character of the
Christian life through a broader description of worship. As the Eucharist
completes initiation into the Christian community and is itself the major
celebration of the paschal mystery, it is an appropriate place to begin.

Eucharistic worship is constituted by four movements: the liturgy of
the Word, the offertory, the Great Thanksgiving, and the communion
and dismissal. First is the proclamation of the Word. Second, in response
to the Word, worshipers offer their prayers and their gifts. In other
words, in response to the Word Christians offer themselves. Third, at
the Great Thanskgiving, expressed in the eucharistic prayer, God accepts
this offering, consecrating and forming the people of God as a holy
community. This formation, the consequence of all that has gone before,
is the fourth movement. As expressed in the prayer of thanksgiving,
accepted and fed we are formed and sent out "into the world in peace
[in wholeness] . . . to love and serve [the Lord] with gladness and
singleness of heart."[10]

This fourfold movement is duplicated at the Great Thanksgiving in
the eucharistic prayer. First is the Word, the narrative of God's action
in the world. Next is the response of the people, the *anemnesis*. This is
more than a remembrance, as the word *anemnesis* is often translated—
"Do this for the remembrance of me."[11] *Anemnesis* is more than an
intellectual recalling. More fundamentally, the worshipers' response to

the proclamation of God's action culminating in Jesus' death and resurrection is to offer themselves to God as Jesus did. In this sense *anemnesis* is a reenactment of Jesus' offering of himself and is thereby an offering of ourselves. God's response to this offering is acceptance and consecration, marked by the invocation of the Holy Spirit (the *epiclesis*) upon the gifts of bread and wine that "they may be the Sacrament of the Body of Christ and his Blood of the new Covenant." This action is concluded in the communion, in sharing in the eucharistic feast.[12]

According to Peter Fink this paschal movement may be described theologically in terms of God's approach, the response to God, God's response, and the consequence. The first movement, God's approach, is expressed by saying grace precedes nature. God is prior to our action. We experience God before we respond. More classically, we would say that God knows us before we know God; we respond always to God's action upon us. We know God through Christ only because the story has been told; and the story is told only because God has first been experienced. God's priority, the fact that the first movement in faith is God's, is clearly illustrated in worship as we begin with the Word of God, read and preached.

The second movement of faith is our response to God. We see the faithful response in Jesus Christ. The response may be described in terms of virtues such as absolute trust and love, humility and obedience, faith and hope, but what is central to the response is that Jesus gave himself to God in the entirety of his life, which reaches its conclusion and fulfillment in his passion and crucifixion. This giving up of himself is nowhere more fully and simply expressed than where in the eucharistic prayer Jesus breaks the bread and takes the cup of wine and gives thanks to God. This simple act of thanks is nothing less than the pure offering of himself.

The third movement of faith is God's response. God does not forget us. As we call out to God and give ourselves to God in all our fear and brokenness, God accepts, remembers and delivers, raises us up, and sends forth his Spirit. "As Jesus was raised up, resurrected, we too are brought from darkness into light, from error into truth, from sin into righteousness, from death into life. The fourth movement [of faith] is the historical realization of it all, the *Christos* made large by the gathering of all humanity into its Christic destiny, realized in sacrament and anticipation as Church, the gathered assembly, the People of God."[13] In other words, the consequence of faith is the church. This is why we

call the church the Body of Christ. The church is not the gathering of
the righteous. The church is nothing other than the paschal mystery
incarnate in the world. The church is the church as it embraces the
paschal mystery of faith itself.

This movement—from God's initiative to our response to God's response
to the consequence in our formation as the people of God—is the paschal
mystery. This movement describes the journey in faith, a journey enacted
in worship that sustains and nurtures faith itself. The problem with the
description of worship to this point is that it has primarily focused on
the words of the liturgy. By focusing on the words of the liturgy, despite
the movement that has been described, there is a tendency to reduce
worship to objective discourse. Such an emphasis would, in the extreme,
reduce faith to objective knowledge and worship to edifying discourse.
True worship, however, enacts the journey in faith. Worship opens
worshipers to acknowledge God's presence and thereby offer themselves
and experience God's grace. In this movement worshipers are changed
and formed into a community of faith. The nature of this movement is
perhaps best indicated by what happens in worship at the nonverbal
level.

In the Eucharist, for example, the liturgy of the Word does more than
tell the story and proclaim the faith. As the story of a people in relation
to God is told—from their experience of creation itself to a sense of the
end of time, from the prophetic outcry, the aphorism of the sage, the
epic story of the priest, the parable of Jesus, to the letters and
proclamations of the early church—the worshipers' preoccupations are
scattered. Private space occupied by individual concerns, as the word
"preoccupation" suggests, is opened. The Word places the world in
perspective. The trivial and commonplace is seen. Worshipers, in a
sense, are silenced and opened to a new world, to God's world. They
may stand in awe and experience a sense of mystery and dependence.
They may feel what has been described as the sacred or holy, that
experience of awe and mystery which both draws them closer and at the
same time creates a sense of fear. Ultimately ineffable, this experience
is the first movement of faith.[14]

The worshipers' response to God enacted in worship is simply to offer
themselves. Far more than time, money, and talents are offered.
Worshipers offer themselves—their needs, concerns, and hopes. This
is explicitly done in the Eucharist in the prayers of the people for the
church and the world, in the confession of sins, and at the offering
itself. Again, this action in response to God is more than cerebral. In

offering alms and oblations worshipers offer their concerns and anxieties, hopes and thanksgivings to God. In truly giving these up to God the worshiper is no longer defined by them. Freed from preoccupation and preconception worshipers experience themselves anew in relation to creation. This is the experience of grace, an experience of fundamental affirmation, what the French call élan vital. Here is the third movement of faith, God's response to our response. This affirmation can only be termed grace since it is not the summation or conclusion of joys, needs, concerns, and hopes but is experienced as prior to them and beyond them. In the Eucharist the experience of affirmation may be sensed at the consecration and perhaps most poignantly upon receiving the bread and the wine. Openness to God may be greatest here as worshipers physically offer themselves before God and wait upon God. God's response is nothing other than God's presence, a grace that passes all understanding, what is called peace or wholeness.

This sense of wholeness completes the movement of faith. In communion the worshiper feels joined with others as a people and at the dismissal—"Go in peace to love and serve the Lord"[15]—feels the sense of affirmation, openness, and care directed back to the world. This is the natural culmination and completion of the movement of faith. In response to God needs, concerns, hopes, and joys are named and offered; opened and silenced the worshiper experiences the grace of God. This fundamental affirmation displaces preoccupations. Worshipers are opened to a new world in which others are accepted for who they are and in which creation itself is embraced. They feel at one with the world beyond, loving it and caring for it. Grace thus transforms human life.

This description of worship is, of course, the description of the most basic movement in life. All of life is first of all dependent upon others. And it is only in opening ourselves to others that we feel related and in touch with them. In this process our worlds grow, enriched and nurtured. The alternative is the atrophy of our world and ultimately the collapse of the self upon itself in death. This is nowhere clearer than in human relationships, illustrated in the relation between parent and child. Children do not create their world; it is given to them as a gift. A natural openness in the child is thereby nurtured and sustained. Deprived of contact with others the child withdraws and may even die. The catatonic child is the most visible example of frustration of this movement. This movement from being acted upon to accepting and opening oneself results in the formation of a person and his or her world.[16]

Worship enacts this movement. Worship is not separate from life in the world. Worship is a symbolic activity. As expressed in the medieval understanding of sacrament, worship effects by signifying.[17] Worship expresses the meaning of life in its ultimate context as it effects that relationship. By this, however, is not meant an activity that simply expresses in a shorthanded manner or aesthetically pleasing form the meaning of our life in the world. As a symbolic activity worship is both mythic and parabolic. Worship expresses the way the world "is," and thereby draws the participant into relation with reality. It also challenges taken for granted attitudes and beliefs about the world that distance individuals from reality. Worship not only expresses the meaning of an individual's life but challenges that life and places the person into a new relation to the world. As individuals worship they are thereby drawn into relationship with God.

When understood in this way, religious faith is not belief but a relationship and way of life which is paschal. As David Power notes, the radical meaning of paschal is expressed in two distinct root metaphors. One centers around the image of *Pascha/Passio*; the other centers around the image of *Pascha/Transitus*. The first image focuses upon the passion itself; the second image focuses on the passage from death to life.[18] Passion literally means to be acted upon, to suffer, and so to experience our limits. In this sense Jesus' passion, which culminates in his death upon the cross, is both the expression of the passion of all human life and the divine response of acknowledgment and acceptance. Passage in turn refers to the movement from Jesus' death to his resurrection and so more broadly the passage from error into truth, sin into righteousness, and death into life. Jesus' response to his passion effects his passage.

The word paschal connotes these two, suffering and passage, in their interrelationship. Through our passion—which is to say the suffering of the limits of our life and ultimately of death itself—is the only means of passage from death to acceptance and reconciliation of our life in the world. In worship this movement to reconciliation is effected as self-concerns are displaced and individuals offer themselves to God. In such offerings the worlds of individuals are opened and enlarged, and they experience the sense of grace by which they are reconciled to the world and impelled to care and embrace the world. This integral relation between suffering and passage is, moreover, expressed in the way in which the images of death and love are so often tied together. The meaning of love may be fully known only in death since death is the ultimate context of our lives and so of both our suffering and our love.

Jesus is the embodiment and revelation of love only as he is reconciled to his death in and through his suffering. [19]

In order for worship to effect the paschal movement of passion and passage the symbols of worship must compel as they communicate. As Victor Turner says, symbols are both "storehouses" of meaning and "powerhouses" that effect such meaning. [20] In this sense worshipers must be able to experience their lives in worship. This is possible because the concreteness of the ritual narrative, action, and environment draws in the worshiper as participant. For example, bread and wine are first of all the staff of life. To take, bless, break, and share bread and wine is among the most fundamental actions of life itself. Unless the ritual action is obscured, the worshiper cannot help but participate in this act. The act draws upon a range of previous experiences, sedimented as they may be in the subconscious. The feeling of dependence is one such feeling that is surely both evoked as well as expressed. Upon this layer is intertwined the narrative of Jesus' passion and resurrection. In the Eucharist the worshiper eats the flesh and drinks the blood of Jesus Christ. In this action the worshiper participates in Jesus' final destiny as her or his own.

Such worship drives the worshiper deeper into life as it makes sense of human life. Certainly as Geertz says, worship, as religion, is a model of reality just as it is a model for reality. [21] Such is the nature of symbols, to give expression to the meaning of a relation or an event and in expressing such meaning to form "the hearers of the word" so that their understanding and actions may more fully express and realize that meaning. Worship like all such symbolic language and action is both descriptive about the way things are and prescriptive about the way things ought to be. [22] In this sense, worship is, as Kavanagh emphasizes, an exchange with reality. [23] It is the way people work out their lives—celebrating and consecrating their lives and thereby dedicating and enabling themselves to more fully realize and deepen their identity.

This understanding of worship is expressed in the meaning of the Christian word for worship, liturgy. The word liturgy comes from the Greek word *leitourgia*, a compound of the word for people (*leitos*, public; *laos*, people) and the word for work (*ergon*). Liturgy originally was not a religious term but referred to public works done at private cost, such as the building of a road, military service offered by citizens, or a drama festival. In translating the Hebrew scripture into Greek the word *leitourgia* was chosen to describe the services of the temple rather than the Greek word that more narrowly designated religious exercises, *orgia* (the English derivative being orgy), which connoted then as now ecstatic rites that were largely private and excessively indulgent. In the New Testament *leitourgia* continued to be used to refer to services in the temple but equally to the ongoing life of the Christian community. Jesus' life and death were understood as "the one liturgy, and Christians whose lives are 'in Christ,' formed and shaped in his likeness, constitute a liturgy also. It would be even better to say that they constitute a working and a making present 'in all time and all place' of the one liturgy."[24] Again, worship and daily life reflect each other, and for Christians this means that both are fundamentally paschal in character.

In one sense, in light of Christian worship, the Christian life flows from faith naturally and spontaneously. We are formed anew in Christ. As Luther emphasized, the Christian life is simply faith active in love. In another sense, however, the Christian life is a matter of choice and struggle. We do not simply become Christians. Rather our relationship with God is an ongoing process of development. We are becoming Christians, and the choices we make either separate us from or drive us deeper into the paschal mystery. The choices we make may create those fortresses that protect us and inhibit our ability to open ourselves to others and to receive God's grace; our relationship to ourselves and between ourselves and others and the rest of creation thereby remains broken. Alternatively, our choices may allow us to acknowledge God, offer ourselves, experience God's grace, and embrace the world.

The task of Christian ethics is to describe the paschal character of life and in this way provide some guidance for individuals so that their lives may more fully be "in Christ." Something of the general character of the Christian life needs to be described. This might be called the Christian stance or perspective and might include a description of the attitudes and dispositions as well as the intentions and purposes that are central to the Christian life.[25] In addition, it is necessary to consider specific situations and particular problems and how individuals may respond in order to express and deepen their identity as Christians. As the paschal understanding of Christian faith and human life is religious, it expresses the fundamental and ultimate character of human life. Human life, though, is lived in the finite and particular. The human struggle is how to conform the particular relations that form human life in accord with the ultimate character of life. What is required is a language that construes the form of these particular relations and frames the specific choices to be made. Moral thought is this language. Ethics then moves from the more general description to the consideration of particular cases.

From the description of worship and Christian faith as paschal something of the character of this life may now be described. This will provide the broader context for considering more specific areas and cases. Most clearly, the character of Christian faith in human life is expressed by the movement from worship to the embrace of the world. In communion with those about us we are called to "go in peace to love and serve the Lord." This movement expresses two central characteristics of the Christian life lived in response to Jesus Christ and witnessed to in the New Testament: a community of love and a community of service.[26] In this sense the dimensions of the paschal liturgy, of our lives in Christ, may be designated in terms of the proclamation of the story of Jesus Christ, fellowship or a community of love, and service or care for those beyond the immediate community of faith. Expressed in Greek these are, respectively, *kerygma*, *koinonia*, and *diakonia*. These three dimensions of faith are integrally related. There can be no proclamation of Christ apart from fellowship and servanthood since fellowship and service are the essential marks of Christ. They bear witness to the Christian proclamation as they mark the life that, on the one hand, flows from faith and, on the other hand, is a life of choice and struggle to drive ourselves deeper in relation to God. Both are necessary.

Fellowship evidences our relatedness to others, dependent upon them in our lives while caring for them in their need. However, without service, without the embrace of those outside our immediate community, our fellowship ceases; it becomes a closed society in which we participate for mutual gain and protection from the world rather than as a community formed from our identity in Christ in which we share ourselves as a moment in the universal embrace of creation itself. Likewise, service requires acceptance and care born amidst the conflict of our daily lives. Without such fellowship service ceases to be a matter of care and compassion and becomes a matter of calculating the needs of others in the abstract. Our world then becomes formed in our own image; when we are unable to achieve the end we envision, our frustrations turn to despair.

Fellowship and service, grounded in response to the Christian story, give some indication of the character of the Christian life. The traditional emphasis on love as agape stands at the center of both. Such a love cares for neighbors, near and far, in their need. This means an openness to those about us and a willingness to embrace what may be troublesome. This is no better reflected than in care for the dying. The dying are always strangers to the living. They confront the living with the one thing which the living cannot have experienced. Care for the dying means above all else being present to them, allowing them to share their fears and anxieties, pain and concerns, and, as importantly, the story of their lives, their loves, and their hopes. Such presence may be known as much in silence as in words. Such care is, moreover, truly paschal as it begins with openness to the other, moving through the mystery of a life to a sense of the gratuitousness of this life to the fullness of compassion. It is because this paschal movement is effected in love that love as agape is so often identified with God. This explains why fellowship and service must have at their heart such a love and why the stranger and those in need have a privileged place in the Christian life.

Such moral images as fellowship, service, and love construe something of the general character of Christian life. More specific images, often contrasting one with another, are necessary to illumine the particular, often conflicting relationships that constitute human life. The development of such a moral language, including the development of norms and principles, is necessary in order to illumine the particularity of human life. This is not to say that the Christian life may be detailed in terms of some set of exceptionless rules that tell what must be done in every human situation. But it is to say that there must be some specifiable form to the Christian life. Without such form Christian worship ceases to make sense and loses its effective power.

Something further of the character of the Christian life and the form of human relations may be suggested. Any attempt to develop a Christian ethic, though, is inevitably abstract if it is not clearly grounded in reflection upon specific issues and relations; therefore, I will ground my understanding of the Christian life in terms of three specific issues— human sexuality and marriage, love and friendship, and the meaning of peace and the use of force. However, before attending to these issues in chapters five, six, and seven I want to expand further the paschal character of the Christian life.

To this point I have described the paschal movement in terms of openness of the self to the world in response to God, the experience of grace, and the consequent embrace and care of creation. Worship effects this movement as it signifies the movement in word and act. Worship and daily life, therefore, must mirror each other if worship is to have any meaning and integrity. Still, it is not altogether clear how grace is effected and so what is the nature of grace and redemption. In part this is because of the lack of attention to sin, to the nature of our separation from God. As disease and remedy are understood in light of each other, redemption is illumined by understanding sin. To this end I want to turn to the church's understanding of sin and reconciliation as it is expressed in the developing forms of the sacrament of reconciliation. The integral relationship between Christian faith and the moral life, and so the central place of Christian ethics in the renewal and deepening of Christian faith, will then become more apparent.

NOTES

1. See the discussion on "essence" in the introduction, p. 18. While acknowledging the infinite play of meanings, this proposal remains liberal as it seeks a critical correlation between the Christian "fact" and human experience. On the method of critical correlation see Tracy, *Blessed Rage for Order*, 32–34. The choice of paschal imagery to construe the character of Christian faith is, as all decisions about primary metaphors, more a conclusion drawn from the variety of investigations that fund this study than a premise established on its own. On the use of metaphors in ethics see Gustafson, *Protestant and Roman Catholic Ethics*, esp. 138–59.

2. The understanding of worship developed here as the primary source of Christian identity reflects the understanding of Aidan Kavanagh and David Power. This stands in contrast with that of Geoffrey Wainwright. For Kavanagh and Power liturgy is fundamentally a transaction with reality grounded in symbolic acts. While appreciating this sacramental perspective, for Wainwright there is a set of beliefs which undergird worship and to which worship gives expression. Worship then is doxological as it gives praise for what God has done. Although Kavanagh, Power, and Wainwright see the interaction between belief and prayer, in the language of sacramental theology Kavanagh and Power emphasize the priority of *lex orandi* (the law of prayer) over *lex credendi* (the law of belief) while Wainwright emphasizes *lex credendi* over *lex orandi*. As Kavanagh explains, *lex orandi, lex credendi* is actually the "tag" for the original patristic maxim *legem credendi lex statuat supplicandi*, the law of belief is founded and constituted by the law of worship. It is wrong, therefore, says Kavanagh, to connect *lex orandi* and *lex credendi* by an "is" and then read in either direction. For Wainwright's position see *Doxology*, 218–83. For Kavanagh's analysis see *On Liturgical Theology*, 122–27. Kavanagh's understanding of worship and liturgy may also be gained, as his position suggests, from an analysis of a specific liturgical rite. See his *The Shape of Baptism* (New York: Pueblo, 1978), esp. 153–201. Also see Power, *Unsearchable Riches*. For a broader discussion of these issues see the

response to Wainwright at the North American Academy of Liturgy in *Worship* 57 no. 4 (July 1983): 290–332.

3. *The Book of Common Prayer*, 364, 379, 363.

4. For a discussion of the meaning of sacrifice see Leonel L. Mitchell, *The Meaning of Ritual* (New York: Paulist Press, 1977), 17–21, 26–28. The classic study in this area remains Royden K. Yerkes, *Sacrifice in Greek and Roman Religions and Early Judaism* (London: A. & C. Black, 1953).

5. Most of the work by liturgists or ethicists on the relation between worship and the moral life or, more specifically, liturgy and ethics has focused on the theology implicit in liturgy, the way in which the acts of worship affect our identity and hence responses in the world, and the disparity between what we confess in worship and what we do in practice. See, e.g., the essays on liturgy and ethics in *Journal of Religious Ethics* 5 no. 2 (Fall 1979): 139–248; William Willimon, *The Service of God: How Worship and Ethics Are Related* (Nashville: Abingdon Press, 1983); Wainwright, *Doxology*, 399–434; and James F. White, *Sacraments as God's Self-Giving* (Nashville: Abingdon Press, 1983), 93–113. My interest, reflecting the work of Kavanagh and Power, is to describe the nature of what happens in worship and thereby develop an understanding of Christian faith and the moral life. My own understanding of liturgy and worship has been informed by the work of anthropologists such as Clifford Geertz and Victor Turner. See Geertz's "Religion as a Cultural System" and "Ethos, World View, and the Analysis of Sacred Symbols," *The Interpretation of Cultures*, 87–125, 126–41. For Turner's views see *The Ritual Process: Structure and Anti-Structure* (Chicago: Aldine Press, 1969). Also important has been Alfred Schutz's phenomenology of the social world. See, e.g., "Symbol, Reality and Society," *Collected Papers*, vol. 1, *The Problem of Social Reality*, ed. Maurice Natanson (The Hague: Martinus Nijhoff, 1971), 287–356. For one description of worship and moral reflection from a Schutzian perspective see Donald E. Miller, "Worship and Moral Reflection," *Anglican Theological Review* 62 no. 4 (October 1980): 307–20.

6. See Mitchell, *The Meaning of Ritual*, 83–86.

7. *The Book of Common Prayer*, 302, 303.

8. Ibid., 306, 307.

9. See Kavanagh, *The Shape of Baptism*, 162, 163.

10. *The Book of Common Prayer*, 365.

11. Ibid., 362.

12. Ibid., 369. See Peter E. Fink, "Investigating the Sacrament of Penance: An Experiment in Sacramental Theology," *Worship* 54 no. 3 (May 1980): 206–20. This fourfold movement may be compared with the fourfold movement Dom Gregory Dix describes as taking, blessing, breaking, and sharing, in *The Shape of the Liturgy* (New York: Seabury Press, 1982; 1st edition, 1945), esp. 743–48. While Dix's account is historical and his categories are different, his understanding of sacrifice as an offering of thanksgiving points to a common understanding of the Eucharist.

13. Fink, "Investigating the Sacrament of Penance," 210.

14. For example, on the holy and the sacred see Rudolf Otto, *The Idea of the*

Holy, trans. John W. Harvey (London: Oxford Univ. Press, 1950); on absolute mystery see Karl Rahner, *Foundations of Christian Faith*, trans. William V. Dych (New York: Seabury Press, 1978), 44–89; on absolute dependence see Friedrich Schleiermacher, *The Christian Faith*, ed. H. R. Mackintosh and J. S. Steward (New York: Harper & Row, 1963), 5–26; and H. Richard Niebuhr, *The Responsible Self*, 108–26.

15. *The Book of Common Prayer*, 366.

16. The description of this movement from displacement to offering, affirmation and wholeness is, broadly speaking, phenomenological. While the description arises from the analysis of the liturgy itself, it reflects other descriptions of the fundamental character of human experience. Two such descriptions are Niebuhr's *The Responsible Self*, esp. 108–45, and Jean Nabert's *Elements for an Ethic* (Evanston, Ill.: Northwestern Univ. Press, 1969).

17. See Karl Rahner, "Introductory Observations," 149–60. More generally, says Rahner, "the Church's worship is not the installation of a primary sacramental sphere in a profane, secular world, it is not an event otherwise without roots in reality, but the explicit and reflex, symbolic presentation of the salvation event which is occurring always and everywhere in the world; the liturgy of the Church is the symbolic presentation of the liturgy of the world" ("On the Theology of Worship," *Theological Investigations* [London: Darton, Longman & Todd, 1983], 19:146). See also, "What Is a Sacrament?" *Theological Investigations* 14:135–48. For a contemporary discussion that grounds such an understanding of sacrament, see Power, *Unsearchable Riches*, esp. 61–82, on the polyvalent character of symbols and their relation to transcendence as both presence and absence.

18. Power, *Unsearchable Riches*, 155. For a broader understanding of suffering in relationship to faith see Richard R. Niebuhr, *Experiential Religion* (New York: Harper & Row, 1972), esp. 43–48, 77, 78.

19. For a psychodynamic description of the relation between love and death see Robert Jay Lifton, *The Broken Connection: On Death and the Continuity of Life* (New York: Simon & Schuster, 1979), 24–35; for a literary description which concludes with the centrality of Jesus in reconciling love and death see Elizabeth Sewell, *The Human Metaphor* (Notre Dame: Univ. of Notre Dame Press, 1964), 159–98.

20. See Victor Turner, *The Forest of Symbols* (Ithaca, N.Y.: Cornell Univ. Press, 1967), 28–30, and the discussion of Turner in Philip W. Turner, "Come, Let Us Eat and Drink: A Meditation on the Revision of *The Book of Common Prayer*," *Anglican Theological Review*, Supplementary Series no. 7 (November 1976): 115–19.

21. As Geertz says, "The acceptance of authority that underlies the religious perspective that the ritual embodies thus flows from the enactment of the ritual itself. By inducing a set of moods and motivations—an ethos—and defining an image of cosmic order—a world view—by means of a single set of symbols, the performance makes the model *for* and model *of* aspects of religious beliefs mere transpositions of one another" ("Religion as a Cultural System," 118). The classic formulation of these issues is that of Emile Durkheim; see Durkheim, *The Elementary*

Forms of the Religious Life, trans. Joseph Ward Slain (London: Allen & Unwin, 1915), e.g., 14, 15, 464, 470, 471.

22. On the nature of human agency and the symbolic character of interpretation, see Schutz, "Symbol, Reality and Society," and Howard L. Harrod, *The Human Center: Moral Agency in the Social World* (Philadelphia: Fortress Press, 1981).

23. See Kavanagh, *On Liturgical Theology*, 88.

24. Charles P. Price and Louis Weil, *Liturgy for Living* (New York: Seabury Press, 1979), 23.

25. See James M. Gustafson who develops what is distinctive about Christian ethics, about how Christian faith affects the moral life, in the various terms of perspective and stance, attitudes and dispositions, purposes and intentions, and norms and principles. See his *Christ and the Moral Life* (New York: Harper & Row, 1968), 238–71, and *Can Ethics Be Christian?* (Chicago: Univ. of Chicago Press, 1975), 38–47, 63–81, 156–58.

26. Margaret Farley suggests a similar framework in "Beyond the Formal Principle: A Reply to Ramsey and Sailer," *Journal of Religious Ethics* 7 no. 2 (Fall 1979): 191–202.

chapter 4

Reconciliation and Christian Community

Christian faith was never a once-and-for-all experience. Whether discussed in terms of the experience of conversion or in terms of justification by grace, reconciliation with God and wholeness of life were never accomplished in some singular moment. The experience of the Christian community has always been that in Baptism and through the Eucharist sin was not entirely defeated. Life after Baptism was not unambiguous. And while the Eucharist was a means of deepening the paschal faith begun in Baptism, rites of reconciliation developed specifically to address the experience of sin and to provide a means of continued reconciliation and so growth in the Christian life. A study of the changes in the rites of reconciliation will provide a fuller understanding of the paschal character of the Christian life and indicate what is morally necessary to effect and sustain this paschal identity.[1]

There were several things the church believed could be done to reconcile those who had fallen back into sin. The prayers of the faithful were believed to be efficacious; martyrs in particular were thought to have the power to enable pardon and reconciliation. The Holy Eucharist as well was seen to provide forgiveness and reconciliation since in the Eucharist the paschal mystery first enacted in Baptism is reenacted. In addition, in the fourth century a rite of penance emerged to deal with serious sin and the notorious sinner, usually those having committed sexual immorality, apostasy, or murder. The Christian guilty of such sins confessed before the bishop or his representative and was banned from full participation in the community, including exclusion from the Eucharist itself. The penitent entered the "order of pentitents"; as a penitent the Christian performed a variety of acts of prayer, mortification, and works of charity. Finally, upon completion of the period of penance of up to several years the penitent was restored to the community of faith in a public celebration, usually on Holy Thursday, signified by the laying on of hands, the kiss of peace, and once again participation in the Eucharist.

The rite was not without its problems. Because of the serious, scandalous character of such sins, public penance was allowed only once. The order of penitents was, moreover, similar to an order of ascetics: prohibitions against military service, the use of the courts, commerce, and sexual relations seem to have been prevalent. Some stigma even remained after public penance. For example, those who had been penitents were generally forbidden to serve as ministers in the community and if married were supposed to remain celibate. In short, to become a penitent was like becoming a monk. It is not surprising that Christians simply postponed penance until their deathbed or else entered a monastic order. By the fifth and sixth centuries public penance declined until it fell from use altogether.

The problem of disciplining a community and of the pastoral response to sinners, of course, remained. In fact, with the influx of "pagan" Europeans into the church with little or no instruction and catechesis and with the widespread adoption of infant baptism, the problem of church discipline and the pastoral response to sinners could only increase. Into this vacuum came a new form of penance and reconciliation called "private" or "tariff" penance. This refers to the practice of privately confessing sins and the assignment of penances, often prayers and fasting for some period of time. These were referred to as tariff penances, from the Italian and Arabic meaning notification, because the penances themselves were noted in handbooks for confessors known as penitential books. In contrast to public confession, tariff penance was more a private matter between penitent and priest and was a rite that could be repeated as often as an individual felt necessary. While changes were made—for example, in 1215 the Fourth Lateran Council required all adults in the Roman Catholic church to make at least an annual confession—this is the rite that the Roman Catholic church and the Anglican church inherited.

Historically what is most interesting is how this very different form of the rite for reconciliation arose, replacing and in fact obliterating the memory of the earlier form of public penance. There is now general consensus that tariff penance arose from Irish penitentials that were used in Irish monasteries for spiritual discipline. Thus if a monk were late to an office a penalty might be imposed. The penitentials were primarily a form of community discipline. It appears that in the late sixth and early seventh centuries this penitential system was introduced in Europe when a large number of Irish monks came to the continent, led by Saint Columban. Thus it seems the tariff penitential system was transplanted from a monastic context to become the discipline for the Catholic church at large.

Nothing would appear to be more different than the public penance of the early church and the private confession that is associated with the Roman Catholic church and, prior to the Second Vatican Council that concluded in 1965, with confessional booths and long lines on Saturday afternoons. Both public penance and private confession, however, intend to reconcile the individual with God and the world by effecting the paschal movement of faith. In response to God both seek to enable individuals to offer themselves to God, to experience God's enduring mercy and grace, and to be reconciled and thereby able to continue as faithful members of the community of faith. The two rites are, though, different because they "combat" different aspects of sin. Understanding these different dimensions of moral evil would clarify the Christian vision of reconciliation and the corresponding way of life that flows from reconciliation and, in turn, deepens and nurtures reconciliation. Paul Ricoeur offers a description of three dimensions of moral evil, of why our actions are not what we intend them to be, of why we do precisely what we will not to do and so become a disgrace to ourselves. As Ricoeur summarizes:

> Instead of the simple experience that one might expect, the confession of sins reveals several layers of experience. "Guilt," in the precise sense of a feeling of the unworthiness at the core of one's personal being, is only the advanced point of a radically individualized and interiorized experience. This feeling of guilt points to a more fundamental experience, the experience of "sin," which includes *all* men and indicates the *real* situation of man before God, whether man knows it or not. It is this sin of which the myth of the fall recounts the entry into the world and which speculation of original sin attempts to erect into a doctrine. But sin, in its turn, is a correction and even a revolution with respect to a more archaic conception of fault—the notion of "defilement" conceived in the guise of a stain or blemish that infects from without. Guilt, sin, and defilement thus constitute a primitive diversity in experience.[2]

Ricoeur's analysis suggests a point of departure in attempting to comprehend the diversity in the history of penance. The different historical forms of penance focus on different dimensions of moral evil and therefore seek different remedies. The hypothesis is provocative in understanding the different rites of penance without creating a historical scheme of that history that would affirm one historical moment only at the expense of another. The history of penance confirms Ricoeur's understanding of the nature of moral evil and thereby illumines the nature of reconciliation and how the paschal movement of faith is effected.

Immanuel Kant said that moral evil is ultimately incorrigible to reason. Evil is radically evil precisely because it is incomprehensible and not within our power to control.[3] Ricoeur refers to this layer of our experience of moral evil as the experience of defilement. We experience evil as something that happens to us; we feel impure, stained, and bound by that which is radically other than ourselves. We experience a sense of death, of fatality.

This most archaic conception of evil is perhaps most difficult for us to acknowledge consciously in the modern world where we tend to view the self as rational and as an agent of self-realization. But certain experiences still bring to consciousness this primordial experience. Sexual seduction gives rise to that sense of defilement and stain even while we also feel a sense of personal responsibility for the breaking of the relations that constitute our human life. A more poignant example is the experience of rape or incest. The sense of personal responsibility is all but gone; the guilt spoken of seems more the experience of shame attached to defilement. Perhaps the most profound experience of defilement, however, is the contemporary experience of war, specifically the war in Vietnam. Those touched by the war experienced the uncleanliness of defilement and the concomitant shunning and rage. What makes this experience so insidious is the lack of any appropriate means of cleansing and reconciliation in our culture. Denial and repression only push the defilement deeper into the psyche; defilement then becomes manifest in dreams, depression, and what to others appear as irrational episodes.[4]

The practice of the early church and the rites of public penance seem especially to engage this element of moral evil, what Ricoeur calls defilement. For those serious sins, capital sins or sins of death, the church saw the sinner as having fallen under the devil, under an alien power, and away from the life-giving power of Jesus Christ. Since such moral evil is not primarily a matter of personal responsibility and the breaking of relations, repentance and forgiveness by the community are insufficient. Rather, the divine order has been desecrated. That order which alone gives life has been defiled. Retribution is thus required in order to reestablish order, to cleanse the stain. In this way the sinner, the one who has fallen under the Evil One, can be reconciled with the community of faith. It is only through such ritual action that reconciliation can be achieved—thus the banning of sinners; the prayers, mortification, and acts of charity required by the order of the penitents; and the final restoration to the community in the rite of public penance. Beyond this, all that the community could do was pray for God's mercy that those who had fallen under the power of the Evil One might come again under the power of God. This is not to say that the early church did not also acknowledge in its ongoing life the other aspects of moral evil. But the dimension of moral evil as defilement seems to dominate the rite of penance in the early church and in that rite appears to overshadow the other dimensions of moral evil.

The response to moral defilement in public penance remains paschal in character. Sinners are confronted by the judgment of the community and their own experience of alienation from themselves as well as from the community. God is in this way experienced as judge; in turn, their own world and preoccupations are radically displaced. The response of the sinner is acknowledgment of guilt. In repentance they join the order of penitents and offer their lives to God. While the discipline may appear severe, it promises to restore the sacred order while reconciling the penitent to that way of life which is marked by the offering of the self unconditionally to God and, correspondingly, embracing the neighbor, especially the stranger. The actual rite of reconciliation celebrated the faith that God does not abandon sinners. God's grace is always present to those who repent and offer themselves to God. The consequence of reconciliation is new life in the community of faith marked by fellowship and service. Such life, moreover, nurtures and sustains reconciliation itself.

The paschal movement required of the notorious sinner is not, however, unique. What is expressed in the rite of public penance expresses the movement in the life of every Christian. This is nowhere more evident than in the central place the Lord's Prayer has held in the community of faith. The community of faith is marked by forgiveness; all are sinners—we ask for forgiveness of our sins as we forgive those who sin against us.[5] All participate in the paschal mystery of judgment, repentance and offering, forgiveness and grace, and newness of life.

For Ricoeur sin is a second dimension of moral evil. This second aspect of moral evil refers to the violation and loss of relation, not simply the relationship with another person but also between the individual and God. The experience of God is not simply that of the divine order but that of a personal ground which gives life to humanity. It is the prophetic tradition in Israel that gives the most explicit voice to this religious dimension of our life and its antithesis in sin. God has initiated a covenant. The gift, which is the gift of life itself, is either acknowledged or rejected. Sin is then fundamentally a refusal, a rebellion, the breaking of our relationship with God. Reconciliation is, therefore, a matter of return to God through acknowledging and accepting the gift of our life. This dimension of moral evil that Ricoeur calls sin seems closer to our consciousness than does the experience of defilement. We have our idols just as did the Israelites: money, social status, our family, tribe, profession, or nation. As we define ourselves by these object-relations we lose ourselves. It is only in relationship with God as the ground of all life that we are given life. Only in a fundamental trust of being itself is reconciliation and new life possible.

The final dimension of moral evil Ricoeur identifies as guilt. In contrast with both sin and defilement, though especially defilement, here is a Copernican revolution in understanding moral evil: instead of falling under the Evil One or breaking a relation, I assume full responsibility for good and hence for evil. While the guilty are captive, they are captive of their own will. Here moral evil has taken on a thoroughly ethical consciousness. The scrupulousness this engenders is not to be despaired; guilt is not to be reduced to the psychological state of feeling guilty for having a guilty conscience, though such is always a danger as witnessed by Paul and Martin Luther. That I am responsible is truly liberating, for in my experience of guilt I know that I am other than my past. Here lies the promise of reconciliation and redemption.

While the early church and especially the rites of public penance engaged the dimensions of defilement—perhaps of necessity since the church's very existence was at stake in the way it handled serious sins and sinners—private confession focuses on moral responsibility (guilt) and the loss of relationship with God and neighbor (sin). This is reflected from the Middle Ages through the present by the theological understanding of penance which emphasizes contrition, confession, satisfaction, and absolution.[6]

Contrition indicates that our past stands over and against what we are meant to be. Our sorrow as well indicates that the past is not something about ourselves which is fated, unchanging, and unredeemable. Sorrow means we feel responsible and hence assumes that we can change. For this reason in private confession sorrow is tied integrally to confession. We feel contrition about particular acts and dispositions that have broken the relationships that form the fabric of our life—hence we confess specific sins. Satisfaction, or penance more narrowly speaking, is not what restores some objective order that has been disordered. Rather, satisfaction is precisely true contrition and confession. Absolution, therefore, came to be given immediately after the confession, and penance was more an act of self-discipline and thanksgiving than an act of retribution.

This theological understanding of the rite of private confession focuses primarily on the dimension of personal responsibility for moral evil, on what Ricoeur has called guilt. This is reflected in the concern in moral theology about the guilty conscience, the scrupulous conscience, the lax conscience, and the ignorant conscience. The reduction of moral evil to individual responsibility and, in turn, to a moralism that results in an individualism is always a danger. Within the form of the sacrament and its ecclesial context both the relationship to God and other people which has been broken and the sense of the divine order which has been abrogated are in principle acknowledged. Contrition and confession arise as our response to our relationship with Christ; they are necessitated by a broken relationship arising from having fallen under a power inimicable to the divine order. In fact, though, moralism and individualism have often been the dominant result of the use made of the liturgical rite of private confession. Still, the paschal character of the rite remains. In naming their sins, penitents offer themselves in response to God. Their trust is that the God who calls for penitence is merciful and accepting, that all that is needed is the acknowledgment of God. Forgiveness and reconciliation, which is to say a restored relationship with God, results in a renewed life.

The meaning of reconciliation and the character of life lived in response to such reconciliation is illumined by the three dimensions of moral evil. Defilement as the desecration of the order of life presupposes an order which gives meaning and wholeness to life. It is only through participation in this way of life that reconciliation is given. Notorious sins—traditionally sexual immorality, apostasy, and murder—threaten the very way of life of the community of faith. Reconciliation for such a sinner to the community of faith can only happen when they no longer threaten the community and, in fact, have become a positive means of support of the community in its way of life. The rite of public penance accomplishes this reconciliation. That there may be ultimate reconciliation apart from the community is a matter beyond the knowledge of the community itself, a matter left to the mercy of God. For the Christian community, however, redemption is never simply a state, moment, or personal relationship. At the heart of Christian faith is a way of life.

The second dimension of moral evil, the dimension of sin, reveals the relationship between the self, God, and the world that is redemptive. Reconciliation cannot be reduced to conformity to the law, to a way of life, but is reconciliation with reality. At the heart of reconciliation is a new relationship with God and the world. Human forgiveness within the community of faith is the experience of acceptance and forgiveness by another person which most often mediates the sense of fundamental affirmation and acceptance that results in the renewal of life and the embrace of the world. Here again, though, the integral relationship between the personal ground of reconciliation and a way of life is evident. To forgive is always to forgive someone for something; forgiveness presupposes a normative way of life and, therefore, a community that is clearly formed in a way of life.

That moral evil is also experienced as a matter of guilt, as something for which I am responsible, cannot stand alone but is necessary in order to make sense out of both the experience of defilement and that of sin. Apart from freedom and responsibility the moral life is reduced to fate, as a way of life into which we are either born or have miraculously entered. A relationship becomes a personal relation, my relationship, only when it is something which I have chosen to enter into, or at least something to which I have consented. Similarly, a way of life is my way of life only when it is something which I have chosen or at least affirmed.

As the three dimensions of moral evil evidence, reconciliation depends upon a community that embodies a distinctive way of life that has at its heart acceptance and forgiveness. Reconciliation cannot be a self-created act of freedom: freedom rests upon being confronted with a vision and way of life that demands a choice and the acceptance and forgiveness that makes such a choice possible. All three dimensions of Christian faith—as a way of life, as forgiveness and grace, and as a matter of freedom—are necessary to make sense of reconciliation in the Christian community. These three dimensions cannot be separated. They are like three strands in a braided rope. The weakening of one of the strands strains and weakens the other strands until the rope itself is frayed and finally breaks.

Among the greatest crises confronting the mainline churches in the modern, pluralistic societies of the West (what have been called the magisterial churches) is the assimilation of the way of life of the Christian community with the society-at-large. Christians become Christian in name only. For such nominal Christians faith is reduced to an individualistic, spiritualistic, and, often within the sacramental traditions, aesthetic experience divorced from any distinctive way of life. Without such a way of life worship becomes a private enclave incapable of challenging the lives of individuals and, in turn, celebrating and effecting a new way of life that reconciles the individual to reality. As the history of reconciliation indicates, understanding Christian faith and redemption in strictly personal and individualistic terms is inadequate. At the most, apart from personal acceptance and participation in a way of life reconciliation is episodic and ephemeral.

The integral relationship between a way of life and the experience of forgiveness and grace reflects the traditional understanding of the relationship between law and gospel.[7] The law functions by convicting humans of their sins and by providing a sense of the direction for their new life. Never, though, does law replace gospel. The law leads to repentance and so opens the individual to the gospel; in turn, the law leads from the gospel in order to nurture that way of life which is attuned and returns to the gospel itself. As the paschal movement of Christian faith is expressed in the Eucharist, the sense of grace leads to an embrace of creation, a sense of oneness with creation, which was expressed in terms of fellowship and service. This indicated already that an understanding of Christian faith in paschal terms cannot be reduced to a movement without content. The paschal movement embodies within itself a moral thrust which animates the movement of faith. While law necessitates gospel, gospel requires law.

In order to effect redemption—a reconciliation that sustains and sanctifies life beyond the initial experience of grace—the paschal character of Christian faith must be expressed and deepened in the relations that form everyday life. The task of Christian ethics is to reflect such a way of life and provide guidance by pairing the paschal character of faith with the more particular relationships of everyday life. Both descriptive and prescriptive, Christian ethics expresses a way of being in the world that will witness and deepen the relationship with God. What is needed is a description that will construe the choices humans confront and will inform their responses in light of the paschal movement. As the paschal image construes the ultimate context of human life, in itself it does not answer the specific questions about what ought to be done in particular situations. In this sense, the moral and the religious are related as part is to whole. The religious construes the ultimate context while the moral construes the particular choices that form the relations of daily life.

The understandings that we have of why we do what we do are as important as the specific choices we make. How we understand our actions expresses our identity and so disposes us to respond in certain ways. The concern of Christian ethics is not to resolve cases as an end in itself. Rather, the description of our lives in light of Christian faith stands at the heart of Christian ethics. Most importantly, Christian ethics should illumine the reasons why Christians respond in certain ways. In this sense, Christian ethics is as much concerned with describing the Christian stance and perspective, attitudes and dispositions, purposes and intentions as developing moral criteria for making specific decisions.[8] Norms, principles, and rules may help to express the form and content of the Christian life, but such descriptions arise and need to be evaluated and applied in light of the broader construing of the Christian life.

As the history of the sacrament of reconciliation makes clear, the need for the formation of a distinctive way of life for the Christian community and the corresponding call for an ethic is not a secondary task of the Christian community. A lively and enduring faith has at its heart a community that is formed "in Christ," in light of the paschal character of the life of Jesus. Worship will itself be renewed only with the restoration of such a way of life. Such a restoration of a way of life at the heart of the Christian community is, of course, an ongoing task requiring both word and deed, vision and action. The development of a Christian ethic that gives expression to this way of life will deepen the sense of what the paschal mystery means and how it is present in human life. In the next three chapters I will focus on human sexuality, friendship and service to the broader community, and the meaning of peace and the use of force in order to develop the form of the Christian life in the personal, social, and political spheres. These concrete moral analyses should illumine specific relations and choices and thereby deepen an understanding of the character of the paschal mystery; they should also indicate the character of an ethic, including the sources necessary to describe a way of life that will illumine everyday life in light of Christian faith.

NOTES

1. For historical accounts of the development of the sacrament of reconciliation from which this summary is drawn see Cyril Vogel, "Sin and Penance," *Pastoral Treatment of Sin*, ed. P. Delhaye, J. Leclercq, et al. (New York: Desclee, 1968), 177–282; and Charles E. Curran, "The Sacrament of Penance Today," *Worship* 43 (1969): 510–31, 590–619; 44 (1970): 2–19; reprinted in Charles E. Curran, *Contemporary Problems in Moral Theology* (Notre Dame, Ind.: Fides, 1970), 1–96. The classic and most detailed study of the sacrament of reconciliation remains Bernard Poschmann, *Penance and the Anointing of the Sick*, trans. Francis Courtney (New York: Herder & Herder, 1964).

2. Ricoeur, *The Symbolism of Evil*, 7, 8.

3. See Immanuel Kant, *Religion within the Limits of Reason Alone* (New York: Harper & Row, 1960), 34–39.

4. See W. Taylor Stevenson, "The Experience of Defilement," *Anglican Theological Review* 64 no. 1 (January 1982): 15–28.

5. See Geoffrey Diekmann, "Reconciliation through the Prayers of the Community," *The Rite of Penance: Commentaries*, ed. Nathan Mitchell (Washington, D.C.: The Liturgical Conference, 1978), 38–49.

6. See Karl Rahner, "The History of Penance," *Theological Investigations* (London: Darton, Longman & Todd, 1983), 15:15, 16, and also "Forgotten Truths Concerning Penance," *Theological Investigations* (London: Darton, Longman & Todd, 1963), 2:153–62.

7. For a recent account on law and gospel see John C. Hoffman's "The Three Uses of the Law," *Ethical Confrontation in Counseling* (Chicago: Univ. of Chicago Press, 1979), 18–30. See also Karl Barth's classic essay, "Gospel and Law," *Community, State and Church*, ed. Will Herberg (Gloucester, Mass.: Peter Smith, 1968), 71–100.

8. See chap. 3, n. 25 above, p. 52.

chapter 5

Effecting the Christian Life

Marriages have varied considerably, both historically and cross-cultur-ally. The expectations for those with clearly defined social roles in traditional societies are in clear contrast to contemporary marriages with their emphasis on mutual support of public vocations and shared responsibilities for home and children. Neither understanding is clearly normative. Each reflects social and economic arrangements of a particular time and community. Moral evaluation requires moving behind the particular arrangement to the form of the relationship, to the way in which husband and wife relate to each other. Only in specifying such forms of life can ethics aid the community of faith in construing the range of choices and aiding its response.

Human sexuality, however, cannot be viewed apart from the broader, underlying vision that frames not only the Christian understanding of sexuality but the more general relationship between humanity and creation. Only in this way can we discern a vision of what our life in light of Christ is meant to be and thereby move from a formal discussion of the task and character of Christian ethics to the content of a Christian ethic grounded in a paschal understanding of Christian faith and human life.

The central moral image in such understanding is that of gift.[1] Such an image is moral as it construes the value of the relationship between individuals and the world about them. As gift describes this relationship between the self and the world, it also prescribes something of the response to which humans are called. Gift expresses the experience of grace that stands at the heart of creation. This is expressed for the

Christian in the creation account where God creates the world and declares that it is good (Gen. 1:1—2:4). And most centrally for the Christian community, the giftedness of life is experienced in worship in the celebration of the paschal mystery with its movement from offering in response to God to the sense of grace to the embrace of creation. Our lives rest upon the initiative of God; our response is offering of ourselves to God; our consequent experience of God's grace renews and impels us into the world to embrace and care for it. More phenomenologically, the paschal movement of life is from absolute dependence to acknowledgment, acceptance and trust to love and fidelity. Gift construes this basic relationship that grounds and constitutes life. Gift reflects the basic truth that John Calvin describes simply as the fact that "we are not our own."[2]

This givenness and giftedness of life in general and of our own personal lives in particular is the basic fact of existence which in worship is celebrated, signified, and effected. We either accept or reject this gift. We thereby either withdraw from the world, attempting to secure some small fortress of security, or else we engage the world, expanding our sense of the world and of our self until the personal self is lost apart from the care of creation. In other words, we atrophy or grow, contract or enlarge as we either accept or reject the gift of life. To accept is to give thanks and to care for our world. To reject is to resent and to demand of the world. The latter response is idolatry, lack of trust that turns the self into the end of life, into a god.

Gift, of course, suggests that the fundamental goodness of creation will insure human fulfillment, that the particular relations and events of human life will bring forth human well-being. This, however, is not the case. The realization of human desire is not by virtue of merit. In turn, suffering is not in accord with human iniquity. The just and innocent suffer, as evidenced by natural disaster, disease, and famine. As Job cries, there is no rational answer to such suffering. James Gustafson argues that the fundamental idolatry of human life, and of the Christian tradition in particular, has been to assume that God and creation were meant for human fulfillment. In contrast, Gustafson claims that while the end of human life is God, human fulfillment is not the final purpose of God. Failure to acknowledge this fact has led to an anthropocentrism which cuts human life off from reality and so makes impossible unconditional praise and thanksgiving. Correspondingly, to acknowledge that human life is not the crown of creation is to accept that life will not yield the maximization of pleasure or the realization of some of the fondest human desires.[3] As the paschal movement of life signifies, reconciliation and new life are inextricably tied to the cross and suffering. While suffering is never an end in itself, it is the means of passage that may purge the self of its own interest and enable the self to experience the pure sense of the gratuitousness of what is, the sense of the blessedness that there is something rather than nothing.

The choice to accept or reject the gift of life is by virtue of human freedom. Humans are created, as expressed in the creation account, in the image of God; like God, humans are able to create. Most of creation— from geological forces to plant and animal life—is reactive to the natural forces, be they physical or biological. Humans, however, are able to image creation. They are able to hold up before themselves what is. In this way they transcend the present and are able to become conscious of themselves and their world. It is because of this self-consciousness that they can acknowledge life as gift. At the heart of such a response is the exuberance of joy, the delight of play, the spontaneity of thanks and praise, and the honor of reverence.[4] The ability to imagine is also the basis for creating new possibilities, for imagining what could be. This capacity to imagine then carries with it not only the glory of being human but also the problem. When the sense of gift is lost, the heart is distorted and with it the image of human life and creation. Imaging life not as gift but in terms of more narrow images of self-fulfillment creates the brokenness we call sin, well expressed as inextricably tied to creation itself in the story of Adam and Eve (Gen. 2:5—3:24).

Freedom and the misuse of freedom carry with them two responsibilities: the responsibility to care for life in its brokenness and the responsibility to prevent the continued misuse of power. To care for life in its brokenness is to love. This is most often understood in terms of comfort and aid to another person, although in a similar fashion we may feel the pains of nature and, in turn, offer our aid. Love in this sense points to further responsibility in a fallen world. Humans have responsibility to rule, to govern so that they may establish an order where the gifts of creation may be honored and nurtured. Of course to address the misuse of power necessitates the concentration of power and therefore the possibility of greater misuse of power and distortions of the order hoped for. In summary, humans are called in response to the gift of creation. They respond first with reverence and care by contemplating and enjoying creation. Second, humans care for creation in its brokenness by caring amidst that brokenness and by working to establish an order where creation may be honored and nurtured.

The distinctive character of the Christian vision with its ground in the sense of the giftedness of the world is heightened by the contrast with the narcissism of contemporary culture, with an ethic where people look at the world in terms of what gives them pleasure and self-fulfillment. As Philip Rieff has graphically expressed it: we are at a time of the triumph of the therapeutic; people seek to be pleased.[5] This turn toward the self as the center of the world is personified in attitudes toward human sexuality. As individuals view sex in terms of self-fulfillment they enter marriage or any sexual relationship as if it were a mutual contract. When the contract is no longer fulfilled then the relationship is void. Hence sex becomes a commodity to be marketed and bargained. The bankruptcy of this understanding is that people are viewed as consumers rather than as persons. Such an understanding leads to the narrowing of our world rather than to its enlargement. Each person must assume a role in order to meet the other person's expectations. In fact, these expectations are highly internalized. Individuals cannot expect someone to meet their expectations unless they too are capable of being the person the other desires. Because the meaning of the relationship is determined by prescribed limits of exchange there is no room for failure, and so there is limited opportunity for self-exploration, self-revelation and discovery, and finally growth and the sense of being truly related.

In contrast, the Christian understands that the individual's life is a gift that awaits discovery rather than a commodity for bargaining and exchange. The notion, for example, that gifts are free, imposing no obligation on the recipient, arises from the market mentality in which all relationships are a matter of contract, unless the contract is suspended as in the case of the gift. In fact, gifts demand a response [6] To accept a gift, to give thanks for a gift, is to care for the gift. If, for example, someone were to see the painting they had given thrown out or mildewed in the basement, the gift would have been rejected and the relationship itself threatened. If in one thing the truth is not told, what else is illusion? If a gift cannot be trusted to the other, can a self be trusted to that person? Trust and vulnerability, acceptance and discovery, are possible only when a gift is honestly received. If someone doesn't like a painting and says so, he or she has honored the relationship and at least made trust possible. The other, the assumed friend, may reject the recipient, especially if the donor's own identity is narrowly defined in terms of his or her work. But the possibility of a relationship in which two people can share themselves, their differences as well as their common beliefs and interests, has been opened. The alternative is to lie, to pretend, and then to shield oneself from the other in order to preserve an illusion. In the end the individual comes to live the lie.

In the Christian vision we become persons only as we are able to accept the other as gift and in response care for that person in trust and openness. Without this acceptance the other is turned into a thing, an object for our self-fulfillment and ultimately our manipulation. We then see the other only in terms of ourselves, and so our world turns in upon itself and atrophies. Unrelated we become suspicious and angry and finally depressed. As T. S. Eliot said,

> There is no life that is not in community,
> And no community not lived in praise of GOD.[7]

Only as we see life itself as a gift and embrace that gift in order to honor it are we able to trust others, remain open to them, and thereby care for them and grow as persons ourselves.

Again, while the primacy of gift in understanding the form of human relationships is for Christians revealed and effected in the paschal movement of Jesus Christ, the image of gift moves beyond the paschal movement itself. Gift is a moral image since it construes our relationship to the world in terms of human response and responsibility. Reverence and care likewise amplify the normative character of human relations. As this evidences, the moral life is not to be identified with the experience of God's grace but rather is the response to the encounter with God in order to express and deepen the relationship with God. In terms of marriage, the Christian must embody this vision of gift and giftedness. Marriage then provides an extended example of the character of the Christian life and the task of Christian ethics.

For the Christian the person someone marries is given, as the individual gives himself or herself, as a gift. Marriage is not a contractual relationship but a gift relationship in which the other is honored and respected, loved and cared for. This has traditionally been called mutuality or the unitive function or end of marriage. In addition, the Christian tradition has understood the purpose of marriage to bear and nurture children. This has traditionally been called the procreative function or end of marriage.[8] These two functions, unitive and procreative, are integrally related. Central to Christian marriage is the conviction that we care for the other not by seeking to fulfill our partner's needs and our own but by joining together in the care and nurture of the broader creation. We are united only as we share in the purposes of creation that reach beyond our immediate perception of needs.

In marriage children have traditionally expressed this broader sense of purpose. Children enter our world as strangers. If we accept and acknowledge them as gifts of God we respect them and give them the freedom to become themselves; our world, in turn, is expanded. If, however, we see children only in our own image, we bind them to us by a conditional love. We love them only as they meet our expectations of what they should do and what they should become. As children seek their own individuality the broader loves that might guide them and solidify their identity are lacking. In order to become themselves the children must rebel against the parent. To the extent that the relationship between parent and child is narrowly bound by a conditional love the rebellion will shatter the relationship. Instead of accepting and honoring their children as gifts that open new opportunities to participate in the world, parents who are themselves bound only by a conditional love find their own worlds closed and ultimately dying.[9]

That marriage must have children to be complete is highly questionable. What is not questionable is that in marriage as in the rest of life we are called to care for and nurture that which stands beyond us but is given to us as gift. Rather than procreative, this end or purpose of marriage is better understood as generative. Bernard Häring proposes the more earthy image of fecundity.[10] In either case, central to marriage is the care for the other by joining together in the care and nurture of the broader creation.

In addition to the unitive and procreative functions of marriage, marriage has also been understood as providing a remedy against sin. Such an evaluation reflects Paul's admonition that if Christians "cannot control themselves, they should marry. Better be married than burn with vain desire" (2 Cor. 7:9, NEB). Sex may express mutuality and generativity, but sex is also a matter of passion and desire. While the negative asceticism of the early church denied bodily desire, more recent evaluations of the tradition have emphasized the positive evaluation of desire.[11] The negative evaluation can only arise when the human self is divided between body and spirit. An embodied self necessitates a positive evaluation of desire. The moral question is not whether desire is good or bad but whether the object of desire is fitting. When sexuality is reduced to pleasure then sex is a commodity and the individual a good or poor purveyor of pleasure. In contrast, when sexuality embraces mutuality and generativity then pleasure is expanded and bodily pleasure is itself a joy that both animates and expresses the love two people have for each other.

The particular vows of a Christian marriage express more specific judgments about the form of marriage necessary in order to nurture and sustain this broader purpose. Traditionally the normative expression of human sexuality has been given in terms of marriage as a monogamous lifelong commitment grounded in public vows. Three components constitute such an understanding of marriage: monogamy, publicity, and vows made for life.[12] From these components have been derived the negative judgments against adultery and polygamy, premarital sexuality, and divorce. In light of the underlying vision of Christian faith and human sexuality, I want to consider these judgments. Foreshadowing the argument, these judgments say more about what we are to become than about condemnation of all but the lifelong monogamous marriage. A vision of the Christian life and human sexuality must give form to our relationships in the world without an idealization and perfectionism which can be tyrannical and crippling. Judgments should rather be seen as the opportunity for people to confront their own lives, to understand how they are truly related to God, and in this way to see what they may become.

As has been emphasized, the sharpest contrast to the Christian understanding of sexual relationships is an understanding that reduces them to a contract. A contract is a conditional relationship: one gives something for something else. If the exchange cannot be fulfilled or the commodity is used up then the contract is null and void. This is the antithesis of what it means to be a person; hence, if our sexuality is to express and nurture what it means to be a person, we must enter into the relationship with no conditional clause. This is most fully expressed in the commitment to love and care for the other until death. To make this vow publicly guards against self-deception and bears witness to a life formed in light of Christian faith.

Monogamy is similarly a norm for Christian marriage. Given the limits within human life, all possibilities cannot be realized. Sexual pleasure needs to be integrated within the values of mutuality and generativity lest these broader purposes be undercut by the pursuit of sexual relations. More than this, though, others also seek not simply sexual pleasure but relationships of care that nurture life in its wholeness. The desire for sexual intercourse as an end in itself is seldom mutual and self-contained. There is no "last tango in Paris"; the desire and end of human life is more than that of Don Juan. In actual history, given the limits of human life, human insecurity and anxiety, and needs and desires for affirmation, monogamy has been the form and witness to care and love in marriage. At their worst polygamy and adultery have turned the other into chattel; at the least they have threatened to compromise the ability of husband and wife to fulfill their vows to love and care for each other.

Whether or not sexual exclusivity is a necessary condition for the mutuality and generativity of marriage may be questioned.[13] Such a judgment rests upon a practical judgment that in light of history reflects an assessment of human possibilities and limits. Certainly sexual intercourse doesn't have a singular meaning across cultures or even within a culture. The judgment that sexual intercourse should only be expressed within monogamous marriage surely reflects the desire to have children raised within a stable family composed of husband and wife. More recently it reflects the romantic view that sexual intercourse expresses the deepest personal communion between people and therefore realizes its full meaning in marriage. Such understandings are historical judgments that reflect an attempt to order a range of goods in human life in order that they may best express and nurture broader meanings. As interpretations of the meaning of human life they cannot be indubitable but can only be developed and argued in terms of the conflicts and relations that form human life.

The purpose of a moral norm is not primarily judicial, rendering final judgment on the morality of specific acts on the basis of immutable moral laws. Rather, norms seek to describe the form of human acts and relations necessary to embody the broader meanings and purposes of life. Deviations from the norm are best not considered narrowly as acts of ignorance or rebellion but as part of a broader conversation about the meaning of human life. Such conversation provides the means of deepening an understanding of what is the most basic meaning of particular acts. At one time, for example, procreation was the only conceivable expression of the broader value of generativity. With the development of successful contraceptives the knot between sexual intercourse and procreation was cut. With the problem of overpopulation there were, moreover, reasons not to bear children. In this light it became possible to discern that the value more fundamental than procreation was that of generativity, of which procreation was then among the most powerful examples.

The moral art of the ethicist is not that of judge in contrast to that of the pastor and spiritual director. Rather, spiritual direction, pastoral care, and moral guidance are all part of the common task of what was traditionally called the "cure of souls." Ascetic theology, pastoral theology, and moral theology are disciplines within the community of faith which seek to envision and form the Christian life. Spiritual understanding and discipline, pastoral care and support, and moral vision and guidance cannot finally be separated. This may be well illustrated in considering divorce.

Divorce first and foremost presents a pastoral crisis. The breakdown of a marriage results from the frustration of the original vow to love and care for the other. As the Orthodox say, in confronting divorce we are confronting the "moral death" of the marriage. In these situations it has become impossible to fulfill the original vow.[14] What is most important pastorally is to help persons understand what has happened and thereby explore the moral reasons for the crisis. In this way the form of life that witnesses and expresses the paschal movement of life may be grasped. Such understanding is essential if there is to be any kind of conversion and reconciliation and so change and growth in light of the crisis, whether the end result is the dissolution of the marriage or its renewal.

Individuals need to understand the expectations they had in the beginning of a marriage—expectations about love, friendship, work, play, children, and all such things which form a relationship. And they need to understand how these developed and changed and, in turn, how the relationship itself turned from love and hope to pain and despair. It is only in coming to such an understanding that people come to understand themselves by confronting otherwise taken-for-granted understandings so that they may reinterpret themselves and their lives in order to begin anew.[15] Pastorally, spiritually, and morally what is most important is not first focusing upon the particular act but helping people describe the crisis they experience. For example, by holding up the broader vision of human sexuality an individual can identify the brokenness in his or her life and gain some sense of the cause of that brokenness. The present situation can then be seen for what it is, both its distance from the normative vision as well as a sense of the directions in which it leads.

For example, while sexual relationships during the separation and the final stages of the death of a marriage reflect the brokenness of human life, it is narrow-minded to focus strictly on the sexual act. Like a premarital sexual relationship, lacking the public vows of life commitment to this specific person, the relationship does not embody the fullness of the Christian vision. It may be based on the need of the moment for acceptance and affirmation. The relationship may be temporary, and at least one person may in the end feel used. Of course, such possibilities exist in marriage as well. Moreover, the relationship may be reconciling and mark the movement forward where sexual desire will express and animate the broader values of mutual care and generativity.

To effect reconciliation and sanctification in our daily lives it is necessary to have the positive, moral vision of how we are to live and form our lives in light of Christian faith. Only a Christian ethic that envisions the Christian response to particular conflicts and relations enables individuals to grasp the choices that they have made and confront them in a fuller or new light. Each such engagement does more than enable a decision. To engage specific decisions and the reasons for these decisions in light of a Christian moral vision is to begin to transform fundamental self-understandings, the reasons for the decisions made in all areas of life. In other words, we are able to tell our stories in Christ only as we are confronted with the positive images that view the choices to be made in our lives in light of the paschal character of reality revealed in Jesus Christ. Only in this way may our stories be revised and transformed as positive journeys in Christ.

The church generally lacks such a coherent, articulated moral vision. This makes moral confrontation, engagement, interpretation, and reinterpretation of individual lives difficult. The problem of a lack of moral vision, moreover, reflects the deeper problem of the lack of a common way of life at the heart of the Christian community. Ethics as reflection upon a way of life is dependent upon that way of life. Like all reflection, ethics presupposes an ethos. In fact, the vision has little or no power to move individuals apart from their participation in that vision as it is embodied in the way of life of a particular community. The problem of a vital ethic grounded in a common way of life in turn reflects the separation between worship and daily life. As worship is the celebration of life grounded in the paschal mystery of Jesus Christ, worship is vitiated, individualized, and spiritualized when it is cut off from a way of life.

The development of the Christian life depends upon the renewal of worship and the life of the community. Christian ethical reflection cannot in itself effect such renewal. Such reflection, however, is essential in order that the paschal mystery may be seen and lived in the relations of daily life. In terms of human sexuality and marriage, the development of such a distinctively Christian ethic depends upon the integration of the broader vision of the Christian life and the particular values of pleasure, mutuality, and generativity in their interrelationship applied to particular relationships and specific practices. This must be expressed and explored, for example, in premarital counseling and marriage counseling, in inquirers' and confirmation classes, and in preaching. In practice, the development of such an ethic probably depends upon a sense of crisis and urgency. Only a crisis in providing pastoral guidance is likely to force the church to engage the theological and ethical tradition on a significant scale. The responsibility for this task begins with the bearers of the tradition and so especially the ordained ministers of the church. The conversation needs to extend to the laity as a whole. As vision must engage reality, the conversation cannot be one-sided.

In the area of human sexuality a frank discussion by Christians about their own sexuality and lifestyles is needed. This needs to happen in the context of acceptance where there is the desire to understand the struggles and difficulties of people today in developing sustaining and nurturing relationships. What is essential for such conversation and the formation of a Christian sexual ethic, however, is engagement with the theological and moral tradition and specifically the values of care and generativity. To seek only to fulfill a particular person is to fall into idolatry; to deny the person for the sake of some grand vision or design is to abstract the self from life in the world and deny the particular relationships that give life. As expressed in Christian marriage, a person's commitment is to care for and nurture the other in the Christian vocation to love and share in creation itself. The vow to the marriage partner is a particular expression of this love and is sustained and realized as the couple is able to share in commitments beyond the marriage itself.

The form of personal relationships which embody and nurture these values of mutuality and generativity will surely vary, for example, for homosexuals and heterosexuals, for singles, and for those who marry. These values, however, are not restricted to marital relations but are central to the Christian life as they witness and nurture the paschal movement of life itself. They express and deepen this paschal movement as they specify how we live out the paschal mystery in the personal relations of daily life. Human life is formed in particular relations, bound as they are by desire; and yet humans are called to a broader world in which all participate. As expressed by the values of mutuality and generativity, both must be honored. To do this is to suffer the dependencies implicit in the paschal image while at the same time being reconciled and drawn more deeply into the broader creation.

NOTES

1. The choice of beginning with the image of gift is informed by the range of sources in understanding Christian faith, from the paschal movement developed in the previous chapters to understanding the moral character of particular relationships. See chap. 3, n. 1 above, p. 49.

2. John Calvin, *Institutes of the Christian Religion*, 2 vols., trans. Ford Lewis Battles (Philadelphia: Westminster Press, 1960), Book III, chap. vi, sect. 1, 690.

3. See Gustafson, *Ethics from a Theocentric Perspective* 1: 88–99, 108–12, 264–74; also see the discussion of suicide in his *Ethics from a Theocentric Perspective*, 2:214–16.

4. Aristotle understood that this was the most basic purpose of human life. He articulated this by saying that the highest virtue, the highest excellence or quality of being human, was contemplation—participating in and enjoying the truth, goodness, and beauty of something simply as it is in itself. See Aristotle, *Nicomachean Ethics*, trans. Martin Ostwald (Indianapolis: Bobbs–Merrill, 1962), 10.7, 1177a–1179b, pp. 286–95.

5. Philip Rieff, *The Triumph of the Therapeutic* (New York: Harper & Row, 1966), 232–61. See also, Richard Sennett, *The Fall of Public Man* (New York: Alfred A. Knopf, 1977), 8–12, 323–336; Christopher Lasch, *The Culture of Narcissism* (New York: W. W. Norton, 1978); and most recently and more positively, Robert N. Bellah et al., *Habits of the Heart: Individualism and Commitment in American Life* (Berkeley: Univ. of California Press, 1985), e.g., 48–51, 276–96.

6. For a discussion of this gift relationship see Paul F. Camenisch, "Gift and Gratitude in Ethics," *Journal of Religious Ethics* 9 no. 1 (Spring 1981): 1–34.

7. T. S. Eliot, "Choruses from the Rock," *The Complete Poems and Plays, 1909–1950* (New York: Harcourt, Brace & World, 1971), 101.

8. On the ends of marriage see Walter Kasper, *The Theology of Christian Marriage*, trans. David Smith (New York: Crossroad Pub. Co., 1980), 8, 15–24; also see Lisa Sowle Cahill, *Between the Sexes: Foundations for a Christian Ethics of Sexuality* (Philadelphia: Fortress Press, 1985), 106, 128, 139–42; and Gustafson, *Ethics from a Theocentric Perspective*, 2:156, 157.

9. See Stanley Hauerwas's discussion of children in "Having and Learning to Care for Retarded Children," *Truthfulness and Tragedy* (Notre Dame: Univ. of Notre Dame Press, 1977), 147–56.

10. Generativity reflects the virtue of adulthood for Erik Erikson. See his *Childhood and Society*, 2d ed. (New York: W. W. Norton, 1963), 266–68. On fecundity see Bernard Häring, *Free and Faithful in Christ*, 3 vols. (New York: Crossroad Pub. Co., 1978–81), 2:516, 517.

11. This has been particularly emphasized by feminist critiques of the spirit/body dualism that has been central to Christianity, resulting in a disembodied spirituality and the denigration of desire. See, e.g., the recent critique by Beverly Wildung Harrison, "Human Sexuality and Mutuality," *Christian Feminism*, ed. Judith L. Weidman (New York: Harper & Row, 1984), 141–57. From the Roman Catholic tradition see the creation-centered spirituality of Matthew Fox in, e.g., *A Spirituality Named Compassion* (Minneapolis: Winston Press, 1979). For Thomas's positive evaluation of passion, see *Summa Theologica* in *Basic Writings of Saint Thomas Aquinas*, ed. Anton C. Pegis (New York: Random House, 1945), 1.2. q. 59, art. 5 in vol. 2, p. 455. Within Protestantism see James B. Nelson, *Embodiment: An Approach to Sexuality and Christian Theology* (Minneapolis: Augsburg Pub. House, 1978).

12. See the marriage vows in *The Book of Common Prayer*, 424. For a recent analysis of these vows see Gustafson, *Ethics from a Theocentric Perspective* 2:177–84.

13. Harrison has argued that given the inordinate expectations for sexual relationships as compensation and support for the isolated male ego in contemporary culture, monogamy only continues to support patriarchy and the broader denial of human sexuality; see "Human Sexuality and Mutuality," 152, 153. I have been significantly influenced by feminist critiques of patriarchal structures and the call for a mutuality grounded in an embodied sense of the human person which is always sexual. At the material level, however, as I have tried to argue here, I have significant reservations about dismissing monogamy as normative for human sexuality. For a discussion of these issues see Nelson, *Embodiment*, and a critique of Nelson by Philip W. Turner, *Sex, Money and Power* (Wilton, Conn.: Morehouse–Barlow, 1985), 29–70, esp. 38–42.

14. For the development of this argument see Philip W. Turner, "The Marriage Canons of the Episcopal Church," *Anglican Theological Review* 65 no. 4 (October 1983): 383; 66 no. 1 (January 1984): 13.

15. For the emphasis on reinterpretation as the basis of freedom and conversion see Niebuhr, *The Responsible Self*, 100–107.

chapter 6

Vocation and the Demands of Love

The development of a Christian ethic that will interpret the Christian life in terms of the paschal movement of faith and thereby deepen that life is often threatened by the conviction that a way of life simply flows spontaneously from faith itself. This "trusting in the Spirit," dominant among some evangelicals and charismatics, is suggested by Paul and Martin Luther when they juxtapose faith and the law. The sum of the Christian life becomes "faith active in love" (Gal. 5:6). Such love is spontaneous and overflowing. Luther expresses this in terms of the freedom of the Christian.[1] With confidence Paul proclaims,

> The harvest of the Spirit is love, joy, peace, patience, kindness, goodness, fidelity, gentleness, and self-control. There is no law dealing with such things as these. And those who belong to Christ Jesus have crucified the lower nature with its passions and desires. If the Spirit is the source of our life, let the Spirit also direct our course. (Gal. 5:22–25, NEB)

However, a close reading of Paul, including placing him in the broader context of the entire New Testament, prevents such a narrow intuitionism. Paul's paschal vision of Christian faith and life—"I have been crucified with Christ; the life I now live is not my life, but the life which Christ lives in me" (Gal. 2:20, NEB)—is detailed by personal narrative and example, by exhortation and judgment, and by further description of both Christian and un-Christian lives.[2] When Paul speaks of love as the character of the Christian life, this is a summary and symbol. Love in itself is an abstraction; alone it cannot express and hence specify the character of the Christian life. Christian identity is given only in the description of a way of life in terms of the conflicts and relations that constitute daily life.

Such a description will not focus narrowly on prescriptions for what ought to be done in specific situations. Rather, ethics must describe how life is to be lived so that it will reflect and deepen the paschal movement in the individual and the community of faith. Such description will indicate a form of life which is normative for the Christian and should provide some practical guidance in making concrete choices. But apart from the broader description that includes the attitudes and dispositions, purposes and intentions that should be embodied in the Christians' relationship to the world, a normative form of life becomes narrow and moralistic.

Human sexuality, for example, reflects and deepens Christian identity only when it expresses the broader values of mutuality and generativity. Such an understanding illumines why certain relations and practices have been normative, such as the monogamous marriage where care between husband and wife is nurtured in the broader embrace of children. It also provides a strong critique of forms of life, such as the sexual partnership founded strictly upon mutual self-fulfillment. However, the understanding of human sexuality developed in the last chapter does not equate the formal values that are integrally related to sexuality with a particular way of life or set of practices. Specific forms of life and practices always reflect other factors that constitute the realm of possibilities. Specific sexual practices will then differ according to the society and the individual.

While specific practices need assessment, they cannot be determined from the formal values themselves. In fact, any such assessment finally rests upon a range of prudential judgments about how certain practices will affect the individual, those directly related to the individual, and the society-at-large. Before particular judgments can be made, the ethical task is to appropriate the tradition critically in order to discern and construe the tensions and conflicts between the relations and values which constitute the world of the individual and the community. In this way the relations and values of daily life may be viewed in relation to the paschal reality so that the actual moral choices and their significance may become apparent.

The Christian understanding of love provides a helpful focus in such visioning of both the tradition and the relations and issues that confront individuals and their relationship to the broader community. Too often love has been understood univocally and as sufficient in itself to mark and guide the Christian life. This has led to an uncritical intuitionism and often the substitution of one aspect of the Christian life for the whole.[3] The critical appropriation of the Christian understanding of love provides a good example of both the essential task of Christian ethics and of the character of the Christian life in view of the paschal mystery of faith. As an extended example I want to develop in this chapter two aspects of love, expressed by the different words of agape and eros, in order to illumine the tensions and develop the form of human relations necessary to witness and deepen the paschal movement in human life.[4]

Love has many meanings. Common usage suggests the diversity: "I love ice cream." "I'm in love." "Love and work are the most important things in life." "Her love for art was unequaled." "They love the street people." The meaning of love is simply not univocal. The Christian tradition has accordingly made many distinctions about different kinds of love and how love is related to other attitudes and dispositions. Using distinctions made in Greek, the most celebrated contrast has been between self-sacrificial love and love that desires to be united with the loved object. The first love, agape, is contrasted with the second, eros.[5]

Agape is universal, nonpreferential, and nonreciprocal. It is the love imaged by God's care for creation—for the lilies of the field and birds of the sky, for the least as much as the advantaged. Such love knows no bounds. Agape is personified by the parable of the Good Samaritan. Such love is expressed by the willingness to lay down one's life for another. In this sense agape is self-sacrificial love, what is traditionally understood as charity.

In contrast, eros is sometimes identified with passion and desire. However, eros should not be identified with the libido as popular conceptions of erotic love would lead us to believe. Bodily desire may be considered in itself. The Greeks, in fact, called such love by a distinct name, *epithymia*. But eros is more than sensuality. Eros is the desire to participate and share in some other reality. In such participation we find our fulfillment. As Plato says in speaking of eros, the one "who loves the beautiful is called a lover because he [or she] partakes in it."[6] In this sense, in contrast to agape, eros is always particular, preferential, and reciprocal.

Friendship has been distinguished as a different form of love which the Greeks called *philia*. As distinct from eros, philia expresses a specific relationship or bond between persons. Such love arises, says

Aristotle, only between equals.[7] Where one person is subservient to another two people cannot share their concerns and hopes, sorrows and joys. In the roles of parent and child, teacher and student, professional and client, worker and apprentice, there may be interest and support, but without equality there will be no friendship. Only equals can know each other and so develop the trust and openness that makes friendship possible. Whether equality is always a matter of our social position and roles or is more fundamentally a matter of our common humanity is a separate question, although this suggests the variety and complexity of friendship.

In all friendship, though, the element of eros is present.[8] From some mutual interest arises love for the individual. From something in common we come to know another person's views on the world, her attitudes, his joys, problems, hopes, and disappointments; sharing in this world we come to care for this person. We don't love the friend for self-gain any more than we love the beautiful for our own sake, but our love for the other person can never be divorced from our common loves. This is why friendship can die by acts of betrayal or infidelity or simply indifference. What has been violated are the commitments we have shared in common, or in the language of love, the loves that have formed our love for each other. Friendship is, therefore, grounded and realized in the integration of our loves with the other person who both shares in these loves and becomes an object of our love. Friendship expresses not so much a love different than eros as the social bond that forms around the loves we have described in terms of eros.[9]

Both philia and eros stand in contrast with agape. While agape is self-sacrificial love of all creation—universal, nonpreferential, and nonreciprocal—both philia and eros are particular, preferential, and reciprocal. We love the good, the true, the beautiful, and correspondingly, this or that friend. The contrast between love as agape and love as eros or philia expresses a fundamental tension in our daily lives, the tension between the universal and the particular.

One response to the tension between agape and eros is to see eros as the natural means that moves us toward agape.[10] Friendship is therefore the school for the universal love we call agape. Love arises from particular relations beginning in the family. Loved, we are able to love. Friendship, while certainly beginning with the particular and conditional, is universal in scope. While on the surface this sounds quite true—and it surely does express a fundamental fact of human life—it is only a partial truth.

To take this perspective exclusively would mean that friends are only means to a greater end, that ultimately it is not the friend we love but the good revealed in and through the friend. Universal love—love for all creation, the outcast and disadvantaged as well as the friend and privileged—may be achieved, but the price is the loss of all particular attachments. When this perspective dominates, the ideal becomes the religious, the monk or the nun who lives a higher way of life by renouncing the world for the service of God.

Alternatively, eros may be seen as the embodiment or incarnation of a more universal and general love. Friendship is a narrowing down of the many towards whom we have goodwill to a few friends whom we particularly choose. From the universalism of agape we move to the attachment and care of eros. Goodwill, what psychologists refer to as the fundamental trust established from early childhood, is never an end in itself. We become friends because of common cares and commitments. We come to love others and commit ourselves to them because the things we are about are integral to persons themselves. Truth, integrity, hospitality, generosity, charity, justice—such virtues do not exist apart from persons. Our commitments can never be to humanity in the abstract; the values we care about only exist in relation to particular individuals.

From this perspective an important truth is gained: we live not as spiritual beings relating to others in formal or abstract ways. We are embodied, incarnate. We live in particular relationships. Only in the concrete relations that form our life are values realized and selves formed. But again, to take this point of view exclusively is slowly but inevitably to allow our particular relations to define our world and so ourselves. We may die for what we love, but we will live and die only for what we believe will further the true, the good, and the beautiful. Once this happens those outside our community are barbarians—the word which derives from the Greek word that literally meant foreigner. In order to avoid an exclusive, cultured Christianity, the claim of agape needs to be heard also. At the heart of Christian faith is the sense of the goodness of what is, the response of trust, and the embrace of creation. The universalism and unconditional character of agape sublates eros. We are not to form our world in order to protect the particular objects loved, but, as the parable of the lost sheep claims, we must be willing to sacrifice all for the sake of the one whom we meet in need.

In order to avoid a spiritualized Christianity, on the one hand, and a cultured Christianity, on the other, the tension between agape and eros must be recognized and maintained. The tension between the two is the tension between a universal love and the particular loves that form human life. Such tension is expressed in such daily questions as: How are we to spend our time in service to the broader community? Will I serve on the committee for the church or accept the request to work for a specific community organization? How should I limit my involvement in order to have time with family and friends and for myself? Should I attend the symphony concert or the bluegrass festival? and, How much time can I take simply to sit and relax? As Samuel Johnson complained of the itinerant preacher John Wesley, "John Wesley's conversation is good, but he is never at leisure. He is always obliged to go at a certain hour. This is very disagreeable to a man who loves to fold his legs and have out his talk, as I do."[11]

An understanding of human life necessitates understanding how human life is lived within this tension between the particular and the universal, between love as desire to participate in the other because of the sense of fulfillment and love as caring for the other, even sacrificing the self for the other, simply because of the ultimate value of the other as other. The distinction between love as agape and eros helps to construe this tension. Ethically this illumines something of the form of the Christian life. This is evidenced by feminists who have argued that previous emphasis on agape, over and against eros, is a masculine response to a male problem that distorts a fuller sense of human reality that limits men and oppresses women. Specifically, when the problem of human life is egocentrism, the exaltation of the self above others and the world, the remedy is loss of self. In other words, when the human problem is pride the remedy is self-sacrifice.[12] This makes sense of male development with its emphasis on autonomy, competitiveness, and independence. In American society, at least, "individual achievement rivets the male imagination, and great ideas or distinctive activity defines the standard of self-assessment and success."[13] However, when the dominant masculine voice of the tradition alone is heard it does not speak to the primary need of women; in fact, it distances women from the very issues essential for them to engage if they are to grow as persons able to love and care.

In contrast to egoism, the fundamental problem for women is the inability to accept themselves. As women develop, the core of their identity is imbedded in the relationships that form their lives. "Sensitive to the needs of others and the assumptions of responsibility for taking care lead women to attend to voices other than their own, to include in their judgment other points of view."[14] This often leads to an unwillingness to judge and to a deference toward others, to the point of self-sacrifice. The problem for women is just the opposite of that of typical men: rather than egocentrism, women have to learn to care for themselves. When care is limited to others their sense of self is lost until there is no one to care. What women need is acknowledgment that self and others are truly interdependent so that care includes themselves.

Destructive is the accusation that human sin is pride and that what is needed is agape as self-sacrifice, particularly to women given a patriarchal culture, narrowing their worlds and their identities by placing them captive to the expectations of others. Friendship as mutual care is, in contrast, necessary in comprehending the experience and need of women. More specifically, eros as the love in which we participate, share, and enjoy and are thereby affirmed and brought to fulfillment as a self is essential if women are to become selves capable of caring for themselves and thereby sustaining their capacity to care for others as well. In order to honor the experiences and the needs of women, Christian ethics cannot focus exclusive attention on the nature and demands of agape. And more broadly, to focus narrowly on agape would not only distort the experiences and needs of women but the needs of men as well.

On a broader social scale, attention to the differences between agape and eros illumine the tension, if not bifurcation, between the private domain and the public realm—in other words, between home and work. Many factors have contributed to this split, especially since World War II. Industrialization, specialization, and professionalization, for example, are three interrelated processes that mark this bifurcation. First, the place of work increasingly has become separate from the place where we live. Work has become concentrated in industrial centers or the office building while, with increased affluence and mobility, people have moved to live in suburban residential areas. Second, entrance into the workforce with the expectation of sufficient earnings to own one's home where one wanted required specialized training and skills, whether apprenticeship or professional education. Third, such specialization resulted in professionalization. Training, interest, location, and the demands of the job bound together automobile workers, truckers, salespeople, accountants, bankers, lawyers, physicians, and professors— to name but some of the myriad of contemporary, specialized professions. Laborers and professionals thereby formed specialized, "professional" groups witnessed by the clearly distinguishable language or jargon that they speak. These different languages are significant. They evidence the diversification and segregation of the workforce. People do not live face-to-face with the full range of laborers that form our common life.

In response to this separation of work from everyday life people have sought personal values and meaning in the family, in friends, and in specialized communities ranging from the church to the athletic club, from the neighborhood school to the theater group. Home and work are split between the private domain and the public realm. Where we dwell—rooted in time and space, nurtured by particular communities and friends—is often at odds with work in the world. Commitment to work, besides leaving little time for personal relations, often demands mobility in order to work and to advance. If our public persona is to be sustained, we learn to keep our private lives tentative and provisional. As Meilaender notes, "The circle soon becomes a vicious one: for those who are enticed by vocational necessities to keep their personal commitments tentative become increasingly isolated and increasingly tempted to try to 'live to work.'"[15]

In this bifurcated world love comes to be understood in terms of service, in doing good for others. What cannot be done through occupation or profession should be done through charity. This sense of love as service reflects the formal characteristics of agape: love which is universal, nonpreferential, and nonreciprocal. In other words, we are to care for all people equally without regard to ourselves. Agape as self-sacrifice becomes the heroic ideal. The home—as with all particular, personal relationships—is viewed as the school for agape. Family and friends provide comfort and support for the work to be done outside the home. When agape so interprets the meaning and end of human life, eros is narrowed to romantic love and eroticism. Eros loses its broader and deeper meaning of love of the good, the true, and the beautiful in which we participate for their own sake. With the loss of mutuality witnessed in friendship, eros is increasingly denigrated and left to the privacy of the home.

Rebellion against this bifurcation is common, of course, as evidenced by romanticism, pornography, and now what is called the culture of narcissism where the cultural ethic is to be pleased. All such movements are, however, reactions against the division of life into public and private where the public realm is valued and the private domain is deprecated. By their singular rejection of the public and their exaltation of the private, they witness to the extent of the division construed by the contrast between agape and eros. The result is a new dualism until there is little left of the self except the episodic.

Theologically and ethically the dimensions of love as both agape and eros must be acknowledged and honored. Both the universality and particularity of love are fundamental to life in the world. The care and intimacy embodied in women's reality and the commitment and labor to form a world that will include all are both essential elements to human life. Luther said it well: the two most important things in human life are love and work. Without care and intimacy there is no self. Without commitments beyond ourselves our world atrophies until the self withers and dies. While particular relations are the school for agape, a universal love is itself only realized in particular relationships. Both of these dimensions of life must be acknowledged and honored. We must love each other, to share and rejoice in each other, in the particular. Such is the nature of eros. Equally, though, we must love and care for all of creation without regard to our fulfillment. Such is the nature of agape.

Ultimately the particular and the universal are not reconcilable, at least if that means understanding one in terms of the other. It is as impossible to turn friendship and eros into the means for realizing agape as it is to make agape a love that leads to friendship and eros. Friendship as the human bond and affection between two particular people and agape as the love of being itself are simply two aspects of human experience that are captured in the broader contrast between eros and agape. The disproportion between these two dimensions of human life, in fact, is the kind of tension and conflict that gives rise to reflection in the first place. The importance of such reflection is that it enables humans to acknowledge the relationships that form human life. The power of such acknowledgment is that it then becomes possible to envision critically and creatively a world in which human life is formed in order to honor these essential dimensions of reality.

For example, understandings of agape and eros raise fundamental questions about the form of the Christian life and the difficulties in forming such a life in contemporary society. In marriage the tension between the love of a particular person and the need to participate in the broader purposes of the world were expressed in terms of the ends of marriage, mutuality and generativity. These two values informed and complemented each other in the context of the marriage relation, the unconditional commitment to "love and to cherish, until . . . parted by death."[16] The form of marriage that brings to fruition mutuality and generativity in their integral relationship is this covenant relationship. There is now, however, no such publicly expressed form of work or friendship. In an earlier age individuals worked according to their "station in life" which was understood as a calling, a vocation. In this smaller scaled world each job seemed necessary for the common good of the community. Family, friends, and work formed an organic network that extended the covenant of marriage into increasingly larger worlds. Now, however, workplaces change and work itself is more often than not measured in terms of private gain. Likewise, while friendships are marked by mutual interest and most often proximity, interests change and individuals move.

An ethic of friendship and vocation is needed to illumine and form the relations that extend beyond the family. At the center of a Christian ethic of friendship will be some understanding of fidelity and constancy. Friendships, like marriage, can only sustain and nurture human life when friends meet regularly and where there is loyalty to the other beyond personal interest and gain. A friend must be more than an acquaintance, such as a fellow worker, shopkeeper, or sports partner.

> Whether child or adult, it is friends who provide a reference outside the family against which to measure and judge ourselves; who help us during passages that require our separation and individuation; who support us as we adapt to new roles and new rules; who heal the hurts and make good the deficits of other relationships in our lives; who offer the place and encouragement for the development of parts of self that, for whatever reasons, are inaccessible in the family context. It's with friends that we test our sense of self-in-the-world, that our often inchoate, intuitive, unarticulated vision of the possibilities of a self-yet-to-become finds expression.[17]

Types of friendships vary, for example, between men, women, men and women, older and younger people, colleagues, neighbors, and former neighbors and associates. Each such friendship provides both opportunities and limitations. Each relation will certainly have its own dynamics. In exploring each of these, something more of the form of friendship would be discerned, a form in which friendship is honored and nurtured as it participates in the broader purposes of the world.

Work and vocation may initially appear even more inaccessible to moral reasoning. An understanding of vocation is far easier in specially formed communities, such as those of the Amish and Mennonites. Work in the society-at-large, however, is not so integrally related to the common good and purposes of a community. The individual's sense of purpose and call is, therefore, difficult to discern and sustain. This reflects, in part, the pluralism of our age. Work is perhaps better visioned in terms of a range of spheres, from locally based economies to multinational corporations, from menial labor to professions that relate both nationally and internationally. Sharing of purposes, education and training, recruitment and selection, evaluation and accountability, collegial support, and compensation necessary to meet basic needs are some of the issues necessary to comprehend in order to understand how individuals are to relate to their work. Only in examining such issues in a range of spheres would it be possible to generalize about patterns necessary to integrate work and purpose. An understanding of vocation would then need to integrate the place of work with an understanding of the purposes and responsibilities given in the communities in which we participate. Questions of stewardship, of the use of one's services and financial resources, must surely be considered in developing such an ethic of work and vocation.

Stewardship, with its emphasis upon our care for the gifts given to us in all of life, might be the place to begin in discerning the form of a Christian ethic of work and vocation. Certainly stewardship suggests the need to attend to the particular relations that constitute our life in the world as both a response and a means of participating in the broader purposes of creation. An ethic of work and vocation, however, can no more be deduced from a broad sense of stewardship than it can from understandings of love as agape and eros. While there is the need for the development of an ethic of friendship and of work and vocation, the primary gain from an analysis of agape and eros has been to discern tensions that are part of the relationships that form human life and to express the general form of the response necessary to express and deepen the paschal mystery of faith.

The importance of the task of ethics to appropriate critically and creatively the past in order to form human life in the world is emphasized with the consciousness that the formation of human life is always expressed and mediated in language. Any vision of human life in the present and for the future depends upon the reinterpretation of the past. In this sense ethics is a discipline with its own history and integrity, informed as it is by the range of sources that interpret the nature of human life and the world.

The understanding of Christian faith in paschal terms—as the offering

of the self in response to God, the experience of the gratuitousness of
what is, and the embrace of the world in fellowship and care—does not
yield an ethic. This movement of faith is rather the fundamental movement
of reality in which all participate from birth to death. This movement,
celebrated and effected in worship, is the basic movement of human
life, the movement that enlarges rather than contracts the world, the
movement of conversion to and reconciliation with creation. The appropriation of this movement into daily life involves a range of activities
such as those traditionally designated as pastoral, spiritual, and moral.
What is distinctive about the moral and ethical is to envision the form
of life that will express and deepen this movement of faith. Central to
this life are the attitudes and dispositions, purposes and intentions that
are expressed by the values of mutual care and generativity as evidenced
in the area of human sexuality and by the understanding of love as agape
and as eros as these illumine the need both to share, participate, and
delight in the other while also embracing the stranger and caring for the
world beyond the self.

To be coherent a Christian ethic moves from primary symbols to
secondary symbols to the more propositional language of norms, principles, and rules. While the paschal image is the root metaphor of
Christian faith itself, the image of gift is a primary moral symbol of
Christian faith. While paschal construes the human relationships to
reality in religious terms, gift construes the fundamental moral dimension
of our relationship to the world, of how in freedom humans should
respond to the world about them. The images of mutual care and
generativity and those of agape, eros, and friendship are then secondary
symbols which image more specific aspects of our relationships in the
world. Norms viewing marriage as a lifelong covenant and the subsequent
formulations of principles and rules regarding such matters as marriage,
divorce, and remarriage are tertiary in that they seek to specify the
particular conditions and actions that would embody the relations that
the secondary symbols construe.

Christian ethics must include the development of norms, principles,
and rules, but these must never alone become the content of Christian
ethics. First it is necessary to develop the basic metaphors and images
that illumine the tensions that constitute human life and suggest the
form of the Christian response. Love, for example, as a singular image
and principle for the Christian life is inadequate precisely because it
abstracts from life and therefore loses the power to illumine and hence

provide guidance. To understand the nature of love as imaged by agape and eros does not resolve the tensions in human life but at least begins to illumine them. More important, it suggests the form of life in faith. As Meilaender says at the conclusion of his study of love and friendship:

> The tension between particular bonds and a more universally open love—of which the tension between friendship and vocation is an instance—cannot be eliminated for creatures whose lives are marked by the particularities of time and place but who yet are made to share with all others the praise of God. The tension between particular and universal love is "solved" only as it is lived out in a life understood as pilgrimage toward the God who gives both the friend and the neighbor.[18]

More sacramentally, the form of the Christian life is imaged in the paschal mystery, in Jesus' passion, crucifixion, and resurrection. Here is the movement of life. Life is a life of suffering, from the original sense of the word meaning to experience the limits impressed by reality. The paschal mystery is that precisely in our suffering the particulars of life and inevitably death, the ultimate mystery of life is encountered, whether it is called God or being or some other name. This encounter requires a no or a yes. We may reject life itself and our world collapses into despair or indulgence. Or we may embrace life and accept it as a gift. If our encounter ends in an embrace and yes, we are transformed and cannot help but love the world and even lay down our lives for the world. Such is the journey of faith, signed and effected in worship.

NOTES

1. "True faith is sure trust and confidence in the heart, and a firm consent whereby Christ is apprehended. . . . Formal righteousness is not charity furnishing and beautifying faith, but it is faith itself. . . . [Good works] flow out of this faith." Martin Luther, *A Commentary on St. Paul's Epistle to the Galatians* (New York: Robert Carter & Brothers, 1856), 135, 138. See also "Treatise on Good Works," *Selected Writings of Martin Luther*, ed. Theodore G. Tappert (Philadelphia: Fortress Press, 1967), 1:103–96 and esp. 112–21; and "The Freedom of a Christian," *Selected Writings of Martin Luther*, 2:9–53.

2. On the necessity of such a contextualist reading of Paul see Paul W. Gooch, "Authority and Justification in Theological Ethics: A Study of 1 Corinthians 7," *Journal of Religious Ethics* 11 no. 1 (Spring 1983): 62–74.

3. The most notable example of such intuitionism is Joseph Fletcher, *Situation Ethics: The New Morality* (Philadelphia: Westminster Press, 1966), which, contrary to the excessive emphasis on self-sacrifice of the Christian tradition (see n. 4 below), led to singular emphasis on self-fulfillment.

4. This discussion stands as a moment in the much broader discussion of understandings of love in the Christian tradition, a discussion that was given particular form by Anders Nygren's study of *Agape and Eros* (Philadelphia: Westminster Press, 1953) in which he opposed the two. For a detailed contemporary account of understandings of agape see Gene Outka, *Agape: An Ethical Analysis* (New Haven: Yale Univ. Press, 1972). My own understanding has been especially informed by the feminist critique of agape (see Barbara Hilkert Andolsen, "Agape in Feminist Ethics," *Journal of Religious Ethics* 9 no. 1 [Spring 1981]: 69–83); by the major historical and philosophical analysis by Irving Singer in *The Nature of Love*, vol. 1, *Plato to Luther*; vol. 2, *Courtly and Romantic* (Chicago: Univ. of Chicago Press, 1984; 1st volume revised and reprinted from 1966); and by Gilbert Meilaender's *Friendship: A Study in Theological Ethics.*

5. See Meilaender, *Friendship*, esp. chaps. 1–3, pp. 6–67.

6. "Phaedrus," trans. B. Jowett in *The Dialogues of Plato* (London: Oxford Univ. Press, 1892), 1:249, 456. See also Singer, *The Nature of Love*, vol. 1, chap. 4, esp. pp. 48–57.

7. For Aristotle's discussion see *Nicomachean Ethics*, bks. 8 and 9, esp. 1158b–1159b, pp. 226–30.

8. For Aristotle's discussion of true friendship, see ibid., bk. 8, 1156b–1157a, pp. 219–21. It is hazardous to distinguish forms of love, specifying stipulative definitions and then relating the various forms. This can too easily obscure the differences that are construed in the different language about love. And yet, there is a tradition of seeing love as one. For a discussion of the forms of love and their unity, see Paul Tillich, *Love, Power and Justice* (New York: Oxford Univ. Press, 1954), 18–34.

9. See Singer, *The Nature of Love*, vol. 1, chap. 5, esp. pp. 88–95.

10. On particular loves as a means toward a universal love and the opposite position, particular loves as the embodiment of a universal love, see Meilaender, *Friendship*, chaps. 1 and 2, pp. 6–35, 38–52. See also Singer, *The Nature of Love*, vol. 1, chaps. 4 and 5, esp. pp. 106–10.

11. Quoted in Meilaender, *Friendship*, 87.

12. See Andolsen, "Agape in Feminist Ethics." For a feminist rethinking of power, activity, and mutuality see Beverly Wildung Harrison, *Making the Connections: Essays in Feminist Social Ethics*, ed. Carol S. Robb (Boston: Beacon Press, 1985), 18–21.

13. Carol Gilligan, *In a Different Voice* (Cambridge: Harvard Univ. Press, 1982), 163.

14. Ibid., 16.

15. Meilaender, *Friendship*, 101.

16. *The Book of Common Prayer*, 436.

17. Lillian B. Rubin, *Just Friends: The Role of Friendship in Our Lives* (New York: Harper & Row, 1985), 13.

18. Meilaender, *Friendship*, 102.

chapter 7

Peace, Poverty, and the Community of Faith

As two extended examples, human sexuality and understandings of love and vocation focused on the personal and social relationships that constitute daily life. Our life, however, is also lived in a social and political world, what the Bible refers to as principalities and powers. A Christian ethic must image our response to this world as much as it does our response to the world of personal and social relations. The images needed to develop a political ethic must also reflect the Christian paschal identity. Here especially, the task of Christian ethics is not to solve the problems of the world but to aid the Christian and the Christian community in forming their lives in such a way that faith is witnessed and nurtured.

Justice has been the primary image of political responsibility. Justice, to give to each what they deserve, demands more than responding to the immediate neighbor. Justice demands responsibility for the social and political order in which we live. The content of the response, however, is not given in the image of justice itself. In order to gain content Christians have often related justice to love as agape.[1] Love expresses unconditional care for each person. Since God loves all, justice demands that all people be treated equally. Certain minimal conditions for all people must be met to insure individual dignity. This would include, for example, food, clothing, shelter, and the opportunity to participate in the social and political order. Differences in opportunities and the distribution of goods could be acceptable only if all members of the society would thereby be advantaged.[2]

For Reinhold Niebuhr, for example, love as agape expresses the very nature of the Christian life. Through Christ we have revealed God's love for us. God's absolute love for humanity calls for the same love from us. We are to love one another, and particularly the least advantaged, without regard to ourselves. Through Christ love as agape becomes an "impossible possibility." The ideal, however, cannot be realized politically where people by nature act according to interest. What is necessary, therefore, is to insure an approximation of love whereby people are at least treated equally.[3] The appeal of such a view of the Christian life is its relative consistency and simplicity. It provides an initial framework for discerning the nature of our responsibilities. Of course, for all those who want to view the Christian life strictly in terms of agape, the price of the singular vision is abstractness. Instead of imaging the variety of tensions in the relationships that form our life in light of Christian faith, the vision becomes an ideal and stands over us as an obligation without the power to move us into new possibilities and relationships.[4]

In the political domain—as in the more personal worlds of family and friends—what is needed are ways of imaging specific conflicts and relations in light of Christian faith. Only in this way will Christian ethics accomplish its task of giving expression to our Christian identity in order to drive us deeper into the paschal mystery. In order to develop this broader understanding of the Christian life and Christian ethics I want to look at the issue of peace. Specifically, I want to summarize the two most significant strands of the Christian tradition, those who have upheld the use of force for the sake of justice and those who have renounced the use of force for the sake of love. The first voice of the tradition has expressed its understanding in terms of what has been called just war theory; the second voice is that of the Christian pacifist. Both nurture values that appear central to human life in light of the paschal mystery, and both suggest relationships between the Christian and those who suffer that would form human life in such a way as to deepen the paschal movement and witness to Christian faith. In light of these two opposing voices, both of which have credence within the Christian tradition past and present, the form of the Christian life can be construed in terms of the meaning of peace itself. Within this broader concern, an analysis of just war theory has the added value of illumining the character, usefulness, and limits of moral norms and principles.

Just war theory is, as its name suggests, concerned with justice in the use of force.[5] The presumption is always to respect human life, never to take innocent life. The taking of human life is at worst the most monstrous of evils since the act negates the possibility of being human. At best the taking of another life is a moral tragedy. But this may be necessary in order to protect innocent life. Just war theory seeks to define the situations in which such use of force is justified. In this sense just war theorists represent a magisterial position, the position of those who assume responsibility to rule the world.

First of all, the use of force and the taking of life has been justified by a just cause. Traditionally three causes have justified waging war and taking human life: (1) to defend the innocent in order to protect them from unjust attack, (2) to restore rights wrongfully denied, and (3) to reestablish a just order. The meaning of respect for life means to protect the innocent. The value of human life would be violated if another's life were allowed to be taken. On the national scale, this was the justification of the United States's entrance into World War II after the bombing of Pearl Harbor. The other two traditional justifications for the use of force—to restore rights and to reestablish a just order—rest upon the claim that to be human is not only to be alive but to be able to live in a world that respects and nurtures individual life. Attacks on human rights, be those rights fundamental human needs such as food and shelter or freedom to speak and assemble, are as much an attack on innocent life as direct assaults on the body. Such attacks must be defended against, even justifying the use of violent force. We find this claim for the use of force in the justification of revolutions, in, for example, the Declaration of Independence which justified the American Revolution.

While the cause may be just, a second criterion or principle necessary to justify the use of deadly force has been that such action is a matter of last resort. To attack another person with the intent to kill when other reasonable measures may still be taken is to undercut the only justification for the use of such force in the first place, the defense of human life. This leads to a third criterion: formal declaration. Declaring one's intent to attack, as in the case of British forces in the Falkland Islands, is the last measure of persuasion short of force itself.

The fourth and fifth criteria are closely related: reasonable hope of success and proportionality. Reasonable hope of success means more than favorable odds of victory. Success means as well that the use of force realizes the values intended. In this sense Jewish resistance in Nazi Germany could be judged reasonable in that the purpose of resistance bore witness to values without which life would be meaningless.

Of course, the problem with this criterion when it is so broadly understood is that it appears to exclude only the most self-indulgent wars. But the point of the criterion is as much to identify the reason for warfare so that it may be debated publicly as it is to delineate a specific condition that must be met in order to justify war.

As the fifth criterion proportionality simply means that the good intended must be proportionate to the evil both prevented and inflicted. War is not justified unless victory promises a better situation, sufficiently better to justify the death of individuals and the disruption and destruction of the social, economic, and political framework of a nation. While a sense of proportion, of the costs of waging a war, is closely related to a judgment about probable success, the criterion of proportionality points more specifically to the need of weighing negative consequences.

Intention itself is also a criterion. Motives such as hatred undercut the right to wage war even if there is a just cause. The sense here is that if war is waged out of hatred or simply retribution then it makes difficult if not impossible the ultimate end of war, to protect the sacredness of life and to establish a just peace.

These six criteria or principles of just war are all directed at the rightness, the justice, of going to war (*jus ad bellum*). Another criterion applies specifically to the conduct in war (*jus in bello*). In order to be just, the means of war must not contradict the purpose of war. The purpose of war is not to kill or to injure the enemy but to restrain them. One kills combatants because they are agents of the enemy state that threatens the innocent; therefore, it is unjustifiable to attack noncombatants or, for that matter, excombatants. To attack such individuals is to attack the very reasons for waging war. This also limits the choice of weapons and the methods of fighting. Both must be in accord with the purpose of waging war and must not undermine these purposes. For example, weapons that cannot distinguish between combatants and noncombatants—such as fire bombs used in the saturation bombing of London and in the bombing of Dresden and Tokyo in World War II— are morally suspect. Guerrilla warfare and terrorism in general are difficult if not impossible to justify for the same reason. Both directly undercut the very values that alone could justify the waging of war.

A final criterion, that war must be waged by a legitimate authority, is a presupposition for the rest of the criteria. Individuals alone do not wage war. Individuals wage war as agents of a state. The obligation to support the state, however, rests upon a just political power. If a political authority is just, citizens confront the presumption that a war is just. If the political order is unjust then its determination of an obligation to wage war is not binding and in fact should be disobeyed since at the most basic level its cause is unjust.

In a rough way these criteria may be ordered lexically.[6] Certain criteria must be met before other criteria are morally relevant. Without a just authority, no justification can be given for war. In turn, without a just cause, concerns about last resort and formal declaration are irrelevant to the justification of waging war. And reasonable hope of success and proportionality become concerns themselves only when all other alternatives have been attempted. Finally, concerns about right intentions and the means of war refer primarily to right conduct in war (*jus in bello*) and so come into primary consideration only if according to the other criteria it is just to go to war (*jus ad bellum*).

Given the advances in military technology since World War II, it is questionable whether total warfare is ever justifiable in the modern world. The distinction between combatants and noncombatants was easy to make when knights rode against each other on open fields. Moreover, in medieval warfare it was pragmatic militarily to abide by such distinctions. Waging war against nearby laborers, destroying lives and fields, in no way aided the military battle and in fact made the success of battle questionable since it would destroy the very resources necessary to provide for the people. In modern warfare, however, there is no clear distinction between combatant and noncombatant. It is difficult to claim that only the soldiers are the combatants. Those producing the armaments are equally waging war; not to attack them is to make success less likely. And it is difficult to distinguish between war industries and the other industries within a nation that, while not specifically directed to the war effort, are still essential to carrying out the war.

Modern means of warfare, especially aerial bombing and nuclear weapons, are incapable of killing only combatants in military areas. Some persons have justified the use of modern weapons, even though it involves increasing numbers of noncombatants, by claiming that the nation as a whole is at war. While some persons are innocent noncombatants, they are never the intended objects of military attack; their death and the destruction of their homes, neighborhoods, and places of work and play are the unintended consequences of attacks directed at military installations. As long as it is unintended, nonmilitary destruction is a tragic consequence of modern warfare but does not make the war in fact unjust. On the one hand, this line of reasoning makes sense. However, such reasoning easily becomes the proverbial slippery slope by which any amount of military destruction can be justified. The broader criterion of proportionality would indicate that there must be some limits. At some point the values which are defended—not only innocent lives but the meaning of life itself—are undermined by the means of warfare.[7] Total nuclear war, for example, is clearly unjustifiable.

Again, it needs to be emphasized these criteria or principles are not so much means of justifying war as means to illumine what must be considered in the moral evaluation of the use of deadly force. These formal criteria raise consciousness about fundamental issues and problems in the use of such force. They presuppose the fundamental equality of all people and the judgment that justice is a precondition of peace. While these convictions may be shared by individuals apart from their religious convictions, for Christians just war criteria also begin to specify the meaning and implications of their faith. They suggest something of the form of the Christian life, of what sort of life arises from and deepens Christian faith.

As formal principles, however, just war criteria are insufficient to vision the Christian life. Such principles delineate the end of action but are unable to express the character of the Christian identity that disposes Christians towards peace. What is needed beyond norms and principles— although it has yet to be developed—is, as the Roman Catholic bishops' pastoral letter on war and peace says, a theology of peace in terms of the biblical understanding of peace as *shalom*, as wholeness.[8]

Something further of the meaning of peace, beyond the protection of the innocent through the use of force as understood by the just war tradition, may be gained by the pacifist tradition as it witnesses to a form of Christian life that self-consciously is grounded in an understanding of peace. As expressed by American pacifist A. J. Muste, "There is no way to peace; peace is the way."[9] In recent Christian ethics Stanley Hauerwas has especially emphasized this point.[10] The character of the Christian life is preeminently marked by peace as the renunciation of violence. This includes the renunciation of power as a means of self-defense; however, such pacifism is not passive in its rejection of violence. The integrity of this stance is in witnessing to the meaning of Christian servanthood by combining the rejection of violence with the embrace and care for those who suffer from violence. This involves solidarity with those who have been violated, expressed most forcefully in care of those who have suffered—feeding the hungry, clothing the naked, and visiting the sick and those in prison.

For the pacifist such renunciation of violence is fundamental to Christian faith because at the core of violence is control, the desire to form the world in our own image. The radical conversion of Christian faith is, therefore, always twofold: the sense of grace in the acknowledgment of God and the turning away from violence. Integrally related, repentance as renouncing violence and accepting God is an ongoing process. Such renunciation does not depend upon effectiveness in history; traditionally it has rested upon the conviction that God acts beyond history, from outside history, and at the end of time will bring judgment upon history and usher in the kingdom of God.[11]

Just war theorists and pacifists seemingly pose irreconcilable responses to the question of the use of force. Just war theorists may defend pacifism as a politically prudent response in certain situations and always as a witness to the unconditional character of Christian faith. Such embraces of pacifism, however, will not reconcile the fundamental differences between the two. The differences may be stated in theological terms, especially the different ways in which pacifists and just war advocates see God in relationship to history. It may, for example, be questioned whether conversion and redemption are necessarily tied to the absolute renunciation of the use of force, especially if God is within history or is the structure of history instead of outside or beyond history. But, more fundamentally, I believe that the different stances are grounded in experiences in different communities with distinctive ways of life. In other words, what grounds the differences between pacifists and just war advocates are the experiences of reconciliation and redemption founded with the different communities of faith.

The power of the pacifist tradition does not arise from its theological assumptions so much as from the integrity of its life. What is proclaimed is embodied in the life of the community, both within the community of faith and in relation to the world. For the pacifist tradition the meaning of peace is expressed positively in the fellowship of believers by the imitation of Jesus' servanthood. The community of the faithful understand themselves as disciples who by taking up the way of the cross become the continuing body of Christ in the world. There is here a sacramental integrity where what is proclaimed is embodied and therefore witnessed in the fellowship of the community and in their broader understanding of themselves as disciples imitating Jesus' servanthood in the world.[12]

The crisis confronting the magisterial church is the lack of such integrity between daily life and worship so that just war theory is abstracted from Christian faith. Without an integral relationship between the life of the Christian community and a broader vision of peace, moral criteria, such as those of just war theory, become irrelevant or simply means of rationalization of current practice. The current lack of a theology of peace reflects the deeper problem of the lack of a clear Christian identity and distinctive way of life which, in turn, further vitiates the power of the church to develop a moral vision and corporate life. Worship reflects this dynamic as it increasingly loses its connection with daily life or becomes a means of consecrating a cultured religion.

This description is surely too one-sided. The proclamation of the gospel has the power to convict and transform. The "dangerous memory of Jesus Christ," as Johann Baptist Metz expresses it,[13] has the power to form Christian community and thereby vitalize worship as well. But what is most difficult is that the power of the gospel stands increasingly over and against the demands of the culture. This opposition needs to be stated as clearly as possible by delineating the character of the Christian life. In this way the gospel story may be proclaimed and lived and so animate understandings of peace and justice. This may be the most difficult, although the most important and constructive, task of Christian ethics.

One suggestive image for the renewal of the Christian life is that of poverty. Gustavo Gutierrez, for example, concludes his *A Theology of Liberation* with a chapter on poverty as the spiritual ground for the Christian life.[14] In the Bible material poverty is scandalous because it robs people of their dignity. Poverty of the spirit, however, is something different. Such poverty—expressed in the prophetic tradition no less than in the Beatitudes—is humility before God, an openness to God where we abandon ourselves and entrust ourselves to God. Such poverty is paschal as it is both a dying to ourselves and a passage to God and those beyond ourselves. Such poverty reflects the giftedness of creation and our response to embrace and nurture the broader creation.

Poverty is such a striking image of the Christian life because it clearly expresses the tension between the Christian vision and that of modern culture and its ethic of pleasure and self-fulfillment. At the material level the disparity between affluence and poverty in the United States and in the world-at-large is scandalous. Poverty is degrading, resulting ultimately in the starvation and death of both the body and the spirit.

In contemporary society as in ancient Israel the poor do not have the means to obtain the basic necessities of life—food, clothing, and shelter. The poor do not simply have less; they do not have the resources necessary to participate in the society. The poor are outcasts. The lack of material goods is not separable from the degradation of the spirit. Within the religious community as within the society as a whole, to be excluded from participation in the community is to lose the sense of a common humanity and therefore the sense of oneself as a person.[15]

What is ironic, however, is that the poor are also viewed in both Hebrew and Christian Scriptures as blessed. The Psalms and the Magnificat (Luke 1:46–55) are powerful expressions of the spiritual power of the poor. Vulnerable, homeless, and powerless, the poor witness to sole dependence upon God. Unable to depend upon their own power or the power of anyone else, the poor throw themselves upon God. Humble, of low estate, the poor are able to welcome God and receive as grace whatever happens. Clearly the poor praised in Hebrew and Christian Scriptures have been nurtured in the community of faith. While dispossessed and alienated, the poor in Scripture still carry with them a longing for God that could only have been given from a community of faith. Such longing also means that they remain members of the community. In fact, the poor consider themselves to be the truly faithful.

Material poverty can no doubt all but destroy any sense of community. Such a situation, reflected in infant deaths from widespread famine, would appear to deny the possibility of any openness to God. In this sense material poverty that excludes an individual from participation in the broader community is always an evil and a scandal to the faithful. However, equally true, spiritual poverty as openness before God is tied to material possessions. It would be less troublesome if the poverty of the spirit blessed in the Gospel of Matthew (5:3–10) could be embraced without the material poverty demanded in Luke (6:20–26). No such simple solution is possible. Bodily desire and need are finally inseparable from an individual's sense of self. Food, clothing, and shelter can never be understood only in terms of bodily needs. They equally express the understanding and aspirations people have of themselves. Bodily need and social status are inextricably intertwined. The use of material goods then becomes an expression of the human spirit and the problem of lust and greed.

Given the range of material wealth between different societies, no simple standard of wealth and poverty is possible. What is required to participate in a nomadic community is different from what is required in an agricultural community, still more from a modern society such as the United States. Some line, however, needs to be drawn that helps distinguish between material possessions necessary for life in community and the consumption of possessions that become ends in themselves. While this has surely always been a problem, it reaches an acute degree in modern societies where acquisition and consumption become the very emblems of citizenship.

Poverty as a mark of the Christian life at the least requires an examination of contemporary lifestyles. Patterns of entertainment and recreation must be examined, as well as the underlying extent to which individuals submit to the inculcation of consumptive values by the media. The meaning of vocation and the choice of work and profession need to be discussed in order to break the bond between worth and financial reward. Perhaps most difficult, the way in which money is used must be considered. That the lives of individuals are highly privatized is no more evident than in this area. Sex is more easily discussed than money. A normative vision for human sexuality is engaged while such a vision governing stewardship is more likely to raise defensiveness and anger.

What is fundamental, however, about such discussions of poverty is that they seek to discover the meaning of peace, of the wholeness of life, beyond individual, personal terms. Such reflection is so difficult because it construes the Christian life in fundamentally social and political terms that place the community of faith in tension with the broader society and culture. Such a critical stance toward the world is inevitable if Christian faith is fundamentally a way of life, paschal in character, that is celebrated and effected in worship. But it is only in the development of such a way of life that the church may become a peaceable community, a community of wholeness that may witness to what all the world is meant to be.

The description of the Christian life in terms of poverty and simplicity moves beyond the paschal movement of faith itself to suggest the form of life that evidences and nurtures this movement. Like pacifism, the emphasis on Christian character and formation may appear to lack realism and relevance. The discussion of poverty and simplicity may appear to have little in common with that of just war theory. It is, however, only when the inner dynamic between the character of the Christian life and the ends of Christian action is developed that an ethic can become an effective resource in Christian formation.

To live simply is to free oneself to hear and respond to the concerns and needs of others. Such experience displaces one's own preoccupations and enables the broader offering and opening of the self. Here grace is experienced, the sense of the goodness and possibilities of life, with the consequent embrace and care of the world. To live simply is to be open to the Spirit of God, to the paschal movement in daily life, which results in a sense of peace marked by hospitality and generosity to those in need. This will not solve the problem of the use of violent force but will form a way of life that is responsive to the cries of justice and the misuse of power. More formal moral considerations, such as just war theory and its application, will have little relevance or effectiveness unless this more difficult task of formation of a common life is addressed. The concern for poverty and simplicity that expresses the peace that faith gives and that animates the drive toward peace in the world is a broader moral description of the Christian life that is needed in the world.

NOTES

1. See Outka, "Agape and Justice," *Agape*, 75–92.

2. See John Rawls's "difference principle" in *A Theory of Justice* (Cambridge: Harvard Univ. Press, 1971), 303.

3. For Reinhold Niebuhr on justice, see *The Nature and Destiny of Man*, vol. 2, *Human Destiny* (New York: Charles Scribner's Sons, 1943), 244–69.

4. Recognizing the rational and calculative character of his understanding of justice, Niebuhr calls for the divine madness of agape: "Justice cannot be approximated if the hope of its perfect realization does not generate a sublime madness in the soul" (*Moral Man and Immoral Society* [New York; Charles Scribner's Sons, 1932], 277).

5. On just war theory, see James F. Childress, "Just-War Criteria," *Moral Responsibility in Conflicts* (Baton Rouge: Louisiana State Univ. Press, 1982), 63–94; David Hollenbach, S.J., *Nuclear Ethics; A Christian Moral Argument* (New York; Paulist Press, 1983); and for a recent review of the literature on the church's response to nuclear warfare, see Allan M. Parrent, "Christians and the Nuclear War Debate," *Anglican Theological Review* 67 no. 1 (January 1985): 67–92.

6. On the ordering of the criteria see Childress, "Just-War Criteria," 82–84.

7. See Paul Ramsey, *The Just War: Force and Political Responsibility* (New York: Charles Scribner's Sons, 1968), 144–47.

8. National Conference of Catholic Bishops, *The Challenge of Peace*, 8, 9.

9. Quoted in Hollenbach, *Nuclear Ethics*, 23.

10. See Stanley Hauerwas, *The Peaceable Kingdom: A Primer in Christian Ethics* (Notre Dame: Univ. of Notre Dame Press, 1983), 72–95.

11. This is especially evident in the classic Anabaptist argument developed by

John Howard Yoder. See his *The Politics of Jesus* (Grand Rapids: Eerdmans, 1972), esp. the final chap., "The War of the Lamb," 233–50.

12. This grounding vision is clearly evident in the early documents of the Anabaptists. See, e.g., "The Schleitheim Brotherly Union," *The Legacy of Michael Sattler*, trans. and ed. John Howard Yoder (Scottdale, Pa.: Herald Press, 1973), 27–54.

13. See Johann Baptist Metz, *Faith in History and Society: Toward a Practical Fundamental Theology*, trans. David Smith (New York: Crossroad Pub. Co., 1980), 88–94.

14. Gustavo Gutierrez, *A Theology of Liberation*, trans. Sr. Caridad Inda and John Eagleson (Maryknoll, N.Y.: Orbis Books, 1973), 287–306.

15. See Michael Walzer, *Spheres of Justice: A Defense of Pluralism and Equality* (New York: Basic Books, 1983), 78–83.

chapter 8

The Necessity of Formation

Central to the argument of this book has been the sense of crisis confronting the church in the United States and the first world in general. Increasingly worship and daily life fail to mirror each other until worship is more mirage than mirror. Too often worship becomes spiritualized, more an aesthetic experience than a community gathered together to celebrate and thereby deepen and nurture a way of life in the world. The decline of participation in the life of the church then reflects poor performances or the lack of cultivated aesthetic consciousness. Or, more fundamentally, such a decline in participation may reflect the disillusionment of people who come to worship seeking salvation and receive something of far less value. To be sure, some churches continue to grow. Largely conservative, these churches grow because they are able to create a seemingly seamless world in which religion consecrates a particular way of life. The power of such communities in the lives of individuals, moreover, often rests with the individual's disaffection with and renunciation of the world beyond the religious community.

While on the one hand, the danger confronting the church is the separation of the sacred and the profane, the professedly religious life and life in the world; on the other hand, the religion of the church can become a sacralization of the profane, the accommodation to a particular culture and hence its blessing. While the first leads to a spiritualized and often aesthetic Christianity, the second leads to a cultural Christianity with a consequent moralism. In the first case Christian faith is separated from the world; in the second Christianity becomes a part of the world. Either response—the spiritualizing or the moralizing of religion—are seemingly universal tendencies within religion. This may well reflect the inevitable tension between the desire for God and that which endures and the fact that human life is constituted in particular relationships in specific communities. The danger of either response, however, is particularly acute in the modern world.

What makes religious faith in the modern world so difficult to sustain with integrity is the voluntary character of the church.[1] In the modern constitutional democracies of the West there is a relatively clear separation of church and state. Instead of established by the state because the church was believed to be the soul of the nation, the church was left as one among a myriad of associations to compete on the marketplace for individual followers. For almost two hundred years in the United States the church remained in a privileged position as the de facto soul of the nation. Only after World War II did the significance and influence of the church wane noticeably. In large measure this reflected the voluntary character of the church.

As a voluntary association the church must attract followers by appealing to their more general interests and convictions. For this reason the church, like all voluntary associations, tends to reflect the larger society and to gradually become assimilated into the broader culture. The church must reflect the world beyond itself in order to attract new members; it must reflect the world of its new members in order to retain them. The strength of voluntary associations, however, is the commitment required of its members. Since one becomes or remains a member by choice rather than by the mandate of the state, the possibility of personal commitment remains high.

As voluntary associations churches have reflected the pluralism and individualism of the culture. New ethnic groups have continued to take root in the United States while rapid technological developments have born cultures of their own. Although the seeds of diversity may have always been present in the church in Western culture, what has happened since World War II, and especially since the 1960s, is that pluralism itself has been acknowledged and embraced. Diverse cultures and ways of life are acceptable and, in fact, to be encouraged so long as they do not infringe upon the rights of others. Especially for the affluent, the ethic has become increasingly individualistic: the individual is bound only by the pursuit of happiness in whatever form that may take. At its extreme this is the culture of narcissism.

For many churches the pluralism and individualism of the culture has led to an aging of their membership who continue their participation because of the legacy of their past. For other churches this has meant the individualization of religion with the promise of personal fulfillment, aesthetic pleasure, or at least worthwhile diversion. For still others there has been a rejection of the culture of pluralism and individualism and in its place an attempt to form a new Christian culture in opposition to the ways of the world of the larger culture. The sociological forces toward pluralism and individualization are taken into the heart of religion or else they are the point of attack by religion. In either case, by accommodation or reaction, pluralism and individualism form the character of the church in the world. In the first case the church becomes increasingly individualistic and disembodied, losing both meaning and power. In the second case the church is increasingly reactionary, idolatrous in its consecration of a particular culture while marginal and irrelevant to the society-at-large.

There is here the haunting sense of decline and decay. The individualization and privatization of human life seems likely only to increase given the forces of modernization. To look in this direction alone is to see an inexorable process in which Christian faith becomes increasingly either accommodated or marginal to the culture and society. In either case, the very faith that mothered Western culture is left to die so that the child may assume its own independence and capacity for self-fulfillment.

In the midst of this crisis, however, the possibility for renewal remains. Positively, the separation of church and state has meant that the church is no longer captive to the state, baptizing individuals into the state as much as into the community of faith. In the West not since before Constantine has the church been independent of the state and so dependent upon its own proclamation and way of life in order to evangelize. From within the community of faith there is quite simply the conviction and hope of faith itself. When, however, we look at our present situation from both perspectives at the same time there is a shudder and the vivid sense that the future is not given but is a matter of choice and action.[2]

My conviction and the argument of this book is that the meaning and power of Christian faith is implacably paschal. Life is given in the particular relations that form our lives. We are fundamentally dependent upon those about us—family, friends, and neighbors—and, as importantly, the natural world that surrounds us. We suffer these relationships

and come either to consent to them, trust in them, and embrace them
or to resent and finally reject them out of the desire to gain self-
sufficiency and ultimately self-fulfillment. But as we did not choose to
be born, we cannot accomplish our final destiny. Attempts at self-
determination fail. To continue to pursue our independence and self-
fulfillment is to fall deeper into sin. Such a way of life breaks the
fundamental relationships of life; the world of the self-proclaimed
autonomous self shrinks, leaving the self ever more isolated and defensive.
The possibility of human life, however, is that in suffering such failure
we are thrown back upon the breadth of relations that constitute and
sustain life. To acknowledge our dependence is the first step to conversion
and reconciliation. In such acknowledgment we open ourselves to the
world about us, experience the gratuitousness of our life together, and
cannot help but embrace and care for the world about us.

This movement is paschal as it is imaged and effected in the paschal
character of Jesus' life, ministry, crucifixion, and resurrection. At the
heart of this movement, as the word paschal denotes, is passion and
passage. Jesus suffered the relations that constitute human life, even as
those brought about his own death. Jesus' consent brought him into full
relationship with the relations that constitute human life, what theologically we call the created order or, more simply, creation. Such
reconciliation stands at the heart of redemption itself. What makes this
story effective for us now, an experience of reconciliation, is that the
church does more than tell the story of Jesus.

The church is the story of Jesus as it lives and celebrates that story
in the world. In worship the paschal faith is enacted. The people do
more than remember or recall the story of Jesus. In worship they enact
the movement of Jesus' life. In hearing the word of God they know that
by their own power they do not constitute life. All of life is dependent
upon the range of relations, known and unknown, that constitute the
world. In response worshipers offer themselves; they open themselves
to God as they offer up their sense of sin, concerns and hopes, praise
and thanksgivings. In such offering the worshiper experiences the sense
of grace, the gratuitousness of life itself. From such grace comes consent
and reconciliation and, in turn, reverence and care for the world in all
its travail.

The primary expressions of such worship, within the sacramental
traditions, are Baptism and Eucharist. As the sacrament of reconciliation
makes clear, however, worship is not a separate activity. Worship has
power only as it celebrates a way of life which for Christians is paschal

in character. Apart from a way of life formed to bear witness and deepen the paschal movement of reality, worship ceases to be more than an individualized, spiritualized exercise, often relegated to the aesthetic domain. Worship and daily life must mirror each other. Only in this way can the faith expressed in worship be in fact celebrated. What is most difficult given the pluralism and individualism of the age is the formation of the community of faith so that daily life is formed in such a way that it actually mirrors what is enacted in worship. Such formation is an essential task of the community of faith. The power of the Christian community to effect the meaning of Jesus Christ in their own lives rests upon being the community proclaimed and celebrated in worship.

Strategies to form the Christian community may vary. Certainly there must be adequate means of learning and appropriating the Christian story. While the recitation and memorization of biblical stories in church schools and adult Bible studies has diminished, there must be some way of engaging the witnesses of faith. In the base communities, the small Christian communities that have become a vital force in the church in Latin America, the reading of the Bible has become the central means of meditation on how God is active in their lives. Similar educational models that combine reflection upon and sharing one's personal experience in light of the Scriptures are effective because they bring together the biblical story and the life of the individual and community. Such action-reflection groups also provide the place where individuals share their lives and can share in the lives of others. Such community nurtures and sustains individuals in offering their concerns and needs, in developing trust and concern for those about them, in accepting their own lives and the opportunities before them, and generally in enlarging their lives and their worlds.

Pastoral care plays an equally central role in Christian formation. Supporting and preparing people at the turning points of life—often celebrated sacramentally as in birth, marriage, and death—provides an opportunity to develop understandings of what is happening and, in turn, to consent and form responses so that Christian faith is deepened. As with biblical study groups, pastoral care needs to be corporate in order to develop and nurture the ongoing life of the community itself and not simply an individual relationship. When done corporately pastoral care enables the community to share and entrust themselves to each other and thereby enables individuals to grow in their ability to embrace and care for those beyond themselves.

Liturgical renewal may also contribute to the formation of the Christian

community. Liturgy as the celebration of the life of the community of
faith in Christ cannot be given a static form; by its very nature liturgical
worship is changing. What was said yesterday means something different
today, even if said in exactly the same way. Liturgies must reflect the
life, beliefs, and idiom of a people. When worship becomes antiquated
it most easily becomes separated from daily life and reduces Christian
faith to a spiritualized or aesthetic realm.

The formation of the Christian community, however, involves more
than sharing together in the community of faith or the renewal of liturgical
worship. To become a community of faith that celebrates a way of life
and thereby deepens that way of life, the community must have at its
center a moral vision that informs and forms the relationships and actions
that constitute the lives of its members. This calls for the development
of an ethic, an ethic that cannot be reduced to a singular principle to
be applied or to a disposition to be cultivated. Rather, the formation of
the Christian community requires that the paschal character of human
reality be related to the particular relationships and actions of everyday
life. For example, sexual relationships are not narrowly matters of
personal fulfillment but confront individuals with another person and
provide the opportunity to care and support our life together in the
broader purposes of creation. The monogamous, lifelong commitments
of marriage limit more immediate desires of pleasure and self-fulfillment
in order to provide the unconditional acceptance and support necessary
to be truly vulnerable, to share failings and possibilities, and, rather
than to fall into another's expectations, to embrace and care for creation
itself.

The development of a Christian ethic requires practical reflection
upon the many relationships that constitute daily life. The meaning of
friendship and, in turn, how we love our friends while we also remain
open to serve the stranger is but one area that demands moral attention.
Similarly the problem of the use of force is a pressing political issue; as
important, though, is the formation of the community that is disposed
to wrestle with the questions of the use of force in order to honor and
care for the innocent. Too often in place of an ethic are broad
generalizations that fail to grasp the primary moral intentions that we
should have in specific situations and, more particularly, how we should
form the relationships that constitute our lives in order that they may
witness and deepen our relationship to the paschal movement of Christian
faith. Preaching, for example, must contain a moral vision if reconciliation

and redemption are not to be reduced to the historical, theological, spiritual, pastoral, and even psychological interpretations that seem to dominate the interpretation of Scripture in preaching. As Christian faith is a way of life, practical moral reflection on the Christian life is essential to the community of faith.

Failure to develop a Christian ethic capable of forming the life of the community will slowly but inevitably undercut the viability of Christian faith in the modern world. Without a way of life that reflects and deepens the paschal movement of life, the community of faith fails to become a community of reconciliation. Without such a way of life reconciliation becomes episodic and ephemeral, and the life of the Christian becomes idolatrous as a particular cultural way of life is substituted for Christian faith itself.

Central to the paschal movement of Christian faith is conversion, the passage from the passions that mark the relationships of our lives to the experience of grace to the embrace and care for creation. God's grace remains eternally available; the question for humans is whether or not they are willing to acknowledge their dependence and, in light of their experience of grace, to open their lives in order to love the world that surrounds them and calls them to enlarge their embrace. No particular form of life can be substituted for this movement of faith, although faith necessarily forms life's relationships. The particular form of sexual relationships, friendships, work and vocation, and the use of force may vary between cultures and individuals. But in order to express and deepen the paschal movement of Christian faith each such area of life must be formed in such a way that the particular demands of the situation are honored while opening up and calling for a broader participation in creation.

Perhaps the most distinguishing mark of the Christian is the willingness to forgive. The centrality of forgiveness is evidenced by the primary place that the Lord's Prayer has had in the church from its beginning.[3] The petition, "forgive us our sins as we forgive those who sin against us," clearly notes that the Christian life is not a matter of perfect obedience to some law of life. In contrast, the Christian community is a body of sinners, those who have failed to fully accept God's grace and embrace the world about them. As sinners who ask for forgiveness and who forgive, Christians acknowledge their continuing dependence, embrace, and openness to those about them. To ask for forgiveness means that the Christian community cannot become self-rightous in substituting their way of life for faith itself. To forgive means that the Christian community does not despair of creation but continues to embrace it and care for it in ever new possibilities.

Forgiveness itself does not mean that the community of faith is a therapeutic community that accepts others without a vision and a way of life of its own. In fact, Christian forgiveness rests upon a way of life. What is too often considered forgiveness is simply tolerance. In contrast, at the heart of Christian forgiveness is an embrace of the other and a call to them to repent of their independence and to share in the joy of God's creation. Christian ethics seeks to give form to our relationships in order to express and nurture such love. An ethic is then both a discipline within the community of faith in order to deepen that faith and an invitation to others to a way of life that is not a matter of law but gospel.

NOTES

1. On the voluntary character of the church, see James M. Gustafson, "The Voluntary Church: A Moral Appraisal," *The Church as Moral Decision-Maker* (Philadelphia: Pilgrim Press, 1970), 109–37. On the context of the voluntary church in the United States as it develops in light of the separation of church and state, see Sidney Mead, *The Lively Experiment* (New York: Harper & Row, 1963), esp. 16–37, 55–71, and *The Nation with the Soul of the Church* (New York: Harper & Row, 1975), esp. 48–77.

2. The broad contours of the description, the sense of crisis, and the turn to the future in terms of faith and commitment reflect the development in the thought of both Ernst Troeltsch and H. Richard Niebuhr as they first critically analyzed the church historically and sociologically and then viewed it theologically. For Troeltsch see *The Social Teaching of the Christian Churches*, trans. Olive Wyon (New York: Harper & Row, 1960; 1st German ed. 1911), 2:1004–13. For H. Richard Niebuhr, see *The Social Sources of Denominationalism* (New York: Henry Holt & Co., 1929), 21–25, 264–84, and *The Kingdom of God in America* (New York: Harper & Row, 1937), ix–xvi, 164–98.

3. See Diekmann, "Reconciliation through the Prayers of the Community."

Bibliography

Andolsen, Barbara Hilkert. "Agape in Feminist Ethics." *Journal of Religious Ethics* 9 no. 1 (Spring 1981): 69–83.

Aquinas, Thomas. *Basic Writings of Saint Thomas Aquinas*. Edited by Anton C. Pegis. New York: Random House, 1945.

Aristotle. *Nicomachean Ethics*. Translated by Martin Ostwald. Indianapolis, Ind.: Bobbs-Merrill, 1962.

Augustine. *Confessions*. Translated by John K. Ryan. Garden City: Doubleday & Co., 1960.

Barth, Karl. "Gospel and Law." *Community, State and Church*. Edited by Will Herberg. Gloucester, Mass.: Peter Smith, 1968, 71–100.

Bellah, Robert N., et al. *Habits of the Heart: Individualism and Commitment in American Life*. Berkeley: University of California Press, 1985.

Book of Common Prayer. New York: The Church Hymnal Corp. and Seabury Press, 1977.

Cahill, Lisa Sowle. *Between the Sexes: Foundations for a Christian Ethics of Sexuality*. Philadelphia: Fortress Press, 1985.

Calvin, John. *Institutes of the Christian Religion*. 2 vols. Translated by Ford Lewis Battles. Philadelphia: Westminster Press, 1960.

Camenisch, Paul F. "Gift and Gratitude in Ethics." *Journal of Religious Ethics* 9 no. 1 (Spring 1981): 1–34.

Childress, James F. *Moral Responsibility in Conflicts*. Baton Rouge: Louisiana State University Press, 1982.

Cochrane, Charles Norris. *Christianity and Classical Culture*. London: Clarendon Press, 1940.

Crossan, John Dominic. *The Dark Interval: Towards a Theology of Story*. Niles, Ill.: Argus, 1975.

———. *In Parables: The Challenge of the Historical Jesus*. New York: Harper & Row, 1973.

111

————. *Raid on the Articulate: Cosmic Eschatology in Jesus and Borges.* New York: Harper & Row, 1976.

Curran, Charles E. *Contemporary Problems in Moral Theology.* Notre Dame, Ind.: Fides, 1970, 1–96.

————. "The Sacrament of Penance Today." *Worship* 43 (1969): 510–31, 590–619; 44 (1970): 2–19.

Diekmann, Geoffrey. "Reconciliation through the Prayers of the Community." *The Rite of Penance: Commentaries.* Edited by Nathan Mitchell. Washington, D.C.: The Liturgical Conference, 1978, 38–49.

Dix, Gregory. *The Shape of the Liturgy.* New York: Seabury Press, 1982; 1st ed. 1945.

Durkheim, Emile. *The Elementary Forms of the Religious Life.* Translated by Joseph Ward Swain. London: Allen & Unwin, 1915.

Eliot, T. S. "Choruses from the Rock." *The Complete Poems and Plays, 1909–1950.* New York: Harcourt, Brace & World, 1971.

Erikson, Erik. *Childhood and Society.* New York: W. W. Norton, 1963.

Farley, Margaret. "Beyond the Formal Principle: A Reply to Ramsey and Sailer." *Journal of Religious Ethics* 7 no. 2 (Fall 1979): 191–202.

Fink, Peter E. "Investigating the Sacrament of Penance: An Experiment in Sacramental Theology." *Worship* 54 (1980): 206–20.

Fisher, David H. "The Pleasures of Allegory." *Anglican Theological Review* 66 no. 3 (July 1984): 298–307.

Fletcher, Joseph. *Situation Ethics: The New Morality.* Philadelphia: Westminster Press, 1966.

Föhrer, Georg. *Introduction to the Old Testament.* Translated by David E. Green. Nashville: Abingdon Press, 1968.

Fox, Matthew. *A Spirituality Named Compassion.* Minneapolis: Winston Press, 1979.

Funk, Robert W. *Parables and Presence.* Philadelphia: Fortress Press, 1982.

Geertz, Clifford. "Ethos, World View, and the Analysis of Sacred Symbols." *The Interpretation of Cultures: Selected Essays.* New York: Basic Books, 1973, 126–41.

————. "Religion as a Cultural System." *The Interpretation of Cultures: Selected Essays.* New York: Basic Books, 1973, 87–125.

————. "Thick Description: Towards an Interpretive Theory of Culture." *The Interpretation of Cultures: Selected Essays.* New York: Basic Books, 1973, 1–30.

Gilligan, Carol. *In a Different Voice.* Cambridge: Harvard University Press, 1982.

Gooch, Paul W. "Authority and Justification in Theological Ethics: A Study in 1 Corinthians 7." *Journal of Religious Ethics* 11 no. 1 (Spring 1983): 62–74.

Gustafson, James M. *Can Ethics Be Christian?* Chicago: University of Chicago Press, 1975.

————. *Christ and the Moral Life.* New York: Harper & Row, 1968.

————. *The Church as Moral Decision-Maker.* Philadelphia: Pilgrim Press, 1970.

————. *Ethics from a Theocentric Perspective.* Vol. 1, *Theology and Ethics*; vol. 2, *Ethics and Theology.* Chicago: University of Chicago Press, 1981, 1984.

Gutierrez, Gustavo. *A Theology of Liberation.* Translated by Sr. Carida Inda and John Eagleson. Maryknoll, N.Y.: Orbis Books, 1973.

Häring, Bernard. *Free and Faithful in Christ.* 3 vols. New York: Crossroad Pub. Co., 1978–81.

Harrison, Beverly Wildung. "Human Sexuality and Mutuality." *Christian Feminism.* Edited by Judith L. Weidman. New York: Harper & Row, 1984, 141–57.

————. *Making the Connections: Essays in Feminist Social Ethics.* Edited by Carol S. Robb. Boston: Beacon Press, 1985.

Harrod, Howard L. *The Human Center: Moral Agency in the Social World.* Philadelphia: Fortress Press, 1981.

Hauerwas, Stanley. *The Peaceable Kingdom: A Primer in Christian Ethics.* Notre Dame, Ind.: University of Notre Dame Press, 1983.

————. "Having and Learning to Care for Retarded Children." *Truthfulness and Tragedy.* Notre Dame, Ind.: University of Notre Dame Press, 1977, 147–56.

Hoffman, John C. *Ethical Confrontation in Counseling.* Chicago: University of Chicago Press, 1979.

Hollenbach, David, S.J. *Nuclear Ethics: A Christian Moral Argument.* New York: Paulist Press, 1983.

Kant, Immanuel. *Religion within the Limits of Reason Alone.* New York: Harper & Row, 1960.

Kasper, Walter. *The Theology of Christian Marriage.* Translated by David Smith. New York: Crossroad Pub. Co., 1980.

Kavanagh, Aidan. *On Liturgical Theology.* New York: Pueblo, 1984.

————. *The Shape of Baptism.* New York: Pueblo, 1978.

Lasch, Christopher. *The Culture of Narcissism.* New York: W. W. Norton, 1978.

Lategan, Bernard C., and Willem S. Vorster. *Text and Reality: Aspects of Reference in Biblical Texts.* Philadelphia: Fortress Press, 1985; Atlanta: Scholars Press, 1985.

Leach, Edmund. *Genesis as Myth and Other Essays.* London: Jonathan Cape, 1969.

Lévi-Strauss, Claude. "The Structural Study of Myth." *Structural Anthropology.* Vol. 1. Translated by Claire Jacobson and Brooke Grundfest Schoepf. New York: Basic Books, 1963, 206–31.

Lifton, Robert Jay. *The Broken Connection: On Death and the Continuity of Life.* New York: Simon & Schuster, 1979.

Luther, Martin. *A Commentary on St. Paul's Epistle to the Galatians.* New York: Robert Carter & Brothers, 1856.

————. "The Freedom of a Christian." *Selected Writings of Martin Luther.* Vol. 2. Edited by Theodore G. Tappert. Philadelphia: Fortress Press, 1967, 9–53.

————. "Treatise on Good Works." *Selected Writings of Martin Luther.* Vol. 1. Edited by Theodore G. Tappert. Philadelphia: Fortress Press, 1967, 103–96.

McFague, Sallie. *Speaking in Parables.* Philadelphia: Fortress Press, 1975.

Maurice, Frederick Denison. *The Kingdom of Christ.* 2 vols. Edited by Alec R. Vidler. London: SCM Press, 1958.

Mead, Sidney. *The Lively Experiment.* New York: Harper & Row, 1963.

Meilaender, Gilbert C. *Friendship: A Study in Theological Ethics.* Notre Dame: University of Notre Dame Press, 1981.

Metz, Johann Baptist. *Faith in History and Society: Toward a Practical Fundamental Theology.* Translated by David Smith. New York: Crossroad Pub. Co., 1980.

Miller, Donald E. "Worship and Moral Reflection." *Anglican Theological Review* 62 no. 4 (October 1980): 307–20.

Mitchell, Leonel L. *The Meaning of Ritual.* New York: Paulist Press, 1977.

Nabert, Jean. *Elements for an Ethics.* Translated by William J. Petrek. Evanston, Ill.: Northwestern University Press, 1969.

National Conference of Catholic Bishops. *The Challenge of Peace: God's Promise and Our Response.* Washington, D.C.: United States Catholic Conference, 1983.

Nelson, James B. *Embodiment: An Approach to Sexuality and Christian Theology.* Minneapolis: Augsburg Pub. House, 1978.

Niebuhr, H. Richard. *Christ and Culture.* New York: Harper & Row, 1951.

———. *The Kingdom of God in America.* New York: Harper & Row, 1937.

———. *Radical Monotheism and Western Culture.* New York: Harper & Row, 1960.

———. *The Responsible Self.* New York: Harper & Row, 1963.

———. *The Social Sources of Denominationalism.* New York: Henry Holt and Co., 1929.

Niebuhr, Reinhold. *Moral Man and Immoral Society.* New York: Charles Scribner's Sons, 1932.

———. *The Nature and Destiny of Man.* Vol. 2, *Human Destiny.* New York: Charles Scribner's Sons, 1943.

Niebuhr, Richard R. *Experiential Religion.* New York: Harper & Row, 1972.

Nygren, Anders. *Agape and Eros.* Translated by Philip S. Watson. Philadelphia: Westminster Press, 1953.

Olafson, Frederick A. *Principles and Persons.* Baltimore: Johns Hopkins University Press, 1967.

Otto, Rudolf. *The Idea of the Holy.* Translated by John W. Harvey. London: Oxford University Press, 1950.

Outka, Gene. *Agape: An Ethical Analysis.* New Haven: Yale University Press, 1972.

Parrent, Allan M. "Christians and the Nuclear War Debate." *Anglican Theological Review* 67 no. 1 (Jan. 1985): 67–92.

Plato. "Phaedrus." *The Dialogues of Plato.* Vol. 1. Translated by B. Jowett. London: Oxford University Press, 1892, 391–489.

Poschmann, Bernard. *Penance and the Anointing of the Sick.* Translated by Francis Courtney. New York: Herder & Herder, 1964.

Power, David. N. *Unsearchable Riches: The Symbolic Nature of Liturgy.* New York: Pueblo, 1984.

Price, Charles P., and Louis Weil. *Liturgy for Living.* New York: Seabury Press, 1979.

Rahner, Karl. *Foundations of Christian Faith.* Translated by William V. Dych. New York: Seabury Press, 1978.

————. "Forgotten Truths Concerning Penance." *Theological Investigations* 2. London: Darton, Longman, & Todd, 1963, 153–62.

————. "Introductory Observations on Thomas Aquinas' Theology of the Sacraments in General." *Theological Investigations* 14. London: Darton, Longman, & Todd, 1976, 149–60.

————. "What Is a Sacrament?" *Theological Investigations* 14. London: Darton, Longman, & Todd, 1976, 135–48.

————. "The History of Penance." *Theological Investigations* 15. London: Darton, Longman, & Todd, 1983, 3–22.

————. "On the Theology of Worship." *Theological Investigations* 19. London: Darton, Longman, & Todd, 1983, 141–49.

Ramsey, Paul. *The Just War: Force and Political Responsibility.* New York: Charles Scribner's Sons, 1968.

Rawls, John. *A Theory of Justice.* Cambridge: Harvard University Press, 1971.

Ricoeur, Paul. "The Question of the Subject." *The Conflict of Interpretations.* Edited by Don Ihde. Evanston, Ill.: Northwestern University Press, 1974, 236–66.

————. *The Symbolism of Evil.* Translated by Emerson Buchanan. Boston: Beacon Press, 1967.

Rieff, Philip. *The Triumph of the Therapeutic.* New York: Harper & Row, 1966.

Rubin, Lillian B. *Just Friends: The Role of Friendship in Our Lives.* New York: Harper & Row, 1985.

Schleiermacher, Friedrich. *The Christian Faith.* Edited by H. R. Mackintosh and J. S. Steward. New York: Harper & Row, 1963.

Scholes, Robert, and Robert Kellogg. *The Nature of Narrative.* New York: Oxford University Press, 1966.

Schutz, Alfred. "Part III/Symbol, Reality and Society." *Collected Papers 1: The Problem of Social Reality.* Edited by Maurice Natanson. The Hague: Martinus Nijhoff, 1971, 207–356.

Sedgwick, Timothy F. "Revisioning Anglican Moral Theology." *Anglican Theological Review* 63 no. 1 (January 1981): 1–20.

Sennett, Richard. *The Fall of Public Man.* New York: Alfred A. Knopf, 1977.

Sewell, Elizabeth. *The Human Metaphor.* Notre Dame: University of Notre Dame Press, 1964.

Singer, Irving. *The Nature of Love.* Vol. 1, *Plato to Luther;* vol. 2, *Courtly and Romantic.* Chicago: University of Chicago Press, 1984.

Smith, John E. *Experience and God.* New York: Oxford University Press, 1968.

Sontag, Susan. "The Aesthetics of Silence." *A Susan Sontag Reader.* New York: Farrar, Straus and Giroux, 1982, 181–204.

Stevenson, W. Taylor. "The Experience of Defilement." *Anglican Theological Review* 64 no. 1 (Jan. 1982): 15–28.

Sykes, Stephen. *The Identity of Christianity.* Philadelphia: Fortress Press, 1984.

Taylor, Jeremy. "Discourse on the Nature and Offices of Friendship." *Works.* Vol. 1. Edited by R. Heber; revised by C. P. Eden. London, 1847.

Tillich, Paul. *Love, Power and Justice.* New York: Oxford University Press, 1954.

Tracy, David. *Blessed Rage for Order.* New York: Seabury Press, 1975.

Troeltsch, Ernst. *The Social Teaching of the Christian Churches.* Translated by Olive Wyon. New York: Harper & Row, 1960.

Turner, Philip W. "Come, Let Us Eat and Drink: A Meditation on the Revision of the Book of Common Prayer." *Anglican Theological Review*, Supplementary Series no. 7 (November 1976): 115–19.

———. "The Marriage Canons of the Episcopal Church." *Anglican Theological Review* 65 no. 4 (October 1983): 371–93; 66 no. 1 (January 1984): 1–22.

———. *Sex, Money and Power.* Wilton, Conn.: Morehouse-Barlow, 1985.

Turner, Victor. *The Forest of Symbols.* Ithaca, N.Y.: Cornell University Press, 1967.

———. *The Ritual Process: Structure and Anti-Structure.* Chicago: Aldine Press, 1969.

Via, Dan O., Jr. *The Parables: Their Literary and Existential Dimensions.* Philadelphia: Fortress Press, 1967.

Vogel, Cyril. "Sin and Penance." *Pastoral Treatment of Sin.* Edited by P. Delhaye, J. Leclercq, et al. New York: Desclee, 1968.

Wainwright, Geoffrey. *Doxology: The Praise of God in Worship, Doctrine and Life.* New York: Oxford University Press, 1980.

Walzer, Michael. *Spheres of Justice: A Defense of Pluralism and Equality.* New York: Basic Books, 1983.

White, James F. *Sacraments as God's Self-Giving.* Nashville: Abingdon Press, 1983.

Wilder, Amos N. *Jesus' Parables and the War of Myths.* Philadelphia: Fortress Press, 1982.

Willimon, William. *The Service of God: How Worship and Ethics Are Related.* Nashville: Abingdon Press, 1983.

Yerkes, Royden K. *Sacrifice in Greek and Roman Religions and Early Judaism.* London: A. & C. Black, 1953.

Yoder, John Howard, editor and translator. *The Politics of Jesus.* Grand Rapids: Eerdmans, 1972.

———. "The Schleitheim Brotherly Union." *The Legacy of Michael Sattler.* Edited by J. H. Yoder. Scottdale, Penn.: Herald Press, 1973, 27–54.

Index of Names